OPPOSING VIEWPOINTS® SERIES

Domestic Violence

Other Books of Related Interest:

Opposing Viewpoints Series

Behavioral Disorders

Chemical Dependency

Male and Female Roles

At Issue Series

Do Children Have Rights?

Violent Children

Current Controversies Series

The Elderly

Prisons

"Congress shall make
no law ... abridging
the freedom of speech,
or of the press."

First Amendment to the US Constitution

The basic foundation of our democracy is the First Amendment guarantee of freedom of expression. The Opposing Viewpoints series is dedicated to the concept of this basic freedom and the idea that it is more important to practice it than to enshrine it.

Domestic Violence

Louise I. Gerdes, Book Editor

GREENHAVEN PRESS
A part of Gale, Cengage Learning

Detroit • New York • San Francisco • New Haven, Conn • Waterville, Maine • London

Elizabeth Des Chenes, *Managing Editor*

© 2012 Greenhaven Press, a part of Gale, Cengage Learning.

Gale and Greenhaven Press are registered trademarks used herein under license.

For more information, contact:
Greenhaven Press
27500 Drake Rd.
Farmington Hills, MI 48331-3535
Or you can visit our Internet site at gale.cengage.com

For product information and technology assistance, contact us at

Gale Customer Support, 1-800-877-4253
For permission to use material from this text or product, submit all requests online at www.cengage.com/permissions

Further permissions questions can be emailed to permissionrequest@cengage.com

Articles in Greenhaven Press anthologies are often edited for length to meet page requirements. In addition, original titles of these works are changed to clearly present the main thesis and to explicitly indicate the author's opinion. Every effort is made to ensure that Greenhaven Press accurately reflects the original intent of the authors. Every effort has been made to trace the owners of copyrighted material.

Cover Image © Michael Blann/Riser/Getty Images.

LIBRARY OF CONGRESS CATALOGING-IN-PUBLICATION DATA

Domestic violence / Louise I. Gerdes, book editor.
   p. cm. -- (Opposing viewpoints)
   Includes bibliographical references and index.
   ISBN 978-0-7377-5719-4 (hbk.) -- ISBN 978-0-7377-5720-0 (pbk.)
   1. Family violence. 2. Family violence--Prevention. I. Gerdes, Louise I., 1953-
   HV6626.D6343 2011
   362.82'92--dc23
                                   2011029880

Printed in the United States of America
1 2 3 4 5 6 7 15 14 13 12 11

Contents

Chapter 2: What Are the Causes of Domestic Violence?

Why Consider Opposing Viewpoints?

> *"The only way in which a human being can make some approach to knowing the whole of a subject is by hearing what can be said about it by persons of every variety of opinion and studying all modes in which it can be looked at by every character of mind. No wise man ever acquired his wisdom in any mode but this."*
>
> John Stuart Mill

In our media-intensive culture it is not difficult to find differing opinions. Thousands of newspapers and magazines and dozens of radio and television talk shows resound with differing points of view. The difficulty lies in deciding which opinion to agree with and which "experts" seem the most credible. The more inundated we become with differing opinions and claims, the more essential it is to hone critical reading and thinking skills to evaluate these ideas. Opposing Viewpoints books address this problem directly by presenting stimulating debates that can be used to enhance and teach these skills. The varied opinions contained in each book examine many different aspects of a single issue. While examining these conveniently edited opposing views, readers can develop critical thinking skills such as the ability to compare and contrast authors' credibility, facts, argumentation styles, use of persuasive techniques, and other stylistic tools. In short, the Opposing Viewpoints Series is an ideal way to attain the higher-level thinking and reading skills so essential in a culture of diverse and contradictory opinions.

In addition to providing a tool for critical thinking, Opposing Viewpoints books challenge readers to question their own strongly held opinions and assumptions. Most people form their opinions on the basis of upbringing, peer pressure, and personal, cultural, or professional bias. By reading carefully balanced opposing views, readers must directly confront new ideas as well as the opinions of those with whom they disagree. This is not to argue simplistically that everyone who reads opposing views will—or should—change his or her opinion. Instead, the series enhances readers' understanding of their own views by encouraging confrontation with opposing ideas. Careful examination of others' views can lead to the readers' understanding of the logical inconsistencies in their own opinions, perspective on why they hold an opinion, and the consideration of the possibility that their opinion requires further evaluation.

Evaluating Other Opinions

To ensure that this type of examination occurs, Opposing Viewpoints books present all types of opinions. Prominent spokespeople on different sides of each issue as well as well-known professionals from many disciplines challenge the reader. An additional goal of the series is to provide a forum for other, less known, or even unpopular viewpoints. The opinion of an ordinary person who has had to make the decision to cut off life support from a terminally ill relative, for example, may be just as valuable and provide just as much insight as a medical ethicist's professional opinion. The editors have two additional purposes in including these less known views. One, the editors encourage readers to respect others' opinions—even when not enhanced by professional credibility. It is only by reading or listening to and objectively evaluating others' ideas that one can determine whether they are worthy of consideration. Two, the inclusion of such viewpoints encourages the important critical thinking skill of objectively evaluating an author's credentials and bias. This evaluation will illuminate an author's reasons for taking a particular stance on an issue and will aid in readers' evaluation of the author's ideas.

It is our hope that these books will give readers a deeper understanding of the issues debated and an appreciation of the complexity of even seemingly simple issues when good and honest people disagree. This awareness is particularly important in a democratic society such as ours in which people enter into public debate to determine the common good. Those with whom one disagrees should not be regarded as enemies but rather as people whose views deserve careful examination and may shed light on one's own.

Thomas Jefferson once said that "difference of opinion leads to inquiry, and inquiry to truth." Jefferson, a broadly educated man, argued that "if a nation expects to be ignorant and free . . . it expects what never was and never will be." As individuals and as a nation, it is imperative that we consider the opinions of others and examine them with skill and discernment. The Opposing Viewpoints series is intended to help readers achieve this goal.

David L. Bender and Bruno Leone,
Founders

Introduction

> *"Domestic violence is a problem that must be dealt with for what it is: a criminal act. The only way to effectively diminish it is through the full force of the criminal justice system, which must treat domestic violence the same as it treats crime by strangers."*
>
> —Kalyani Robbins,
> *professor of law,*
> *University of Akron School of Law*

> *"Criminal justice intervention [in domestic violence cases] has produced troubling results for individual victims, the communities in which they live, and the domestic violence movement generally."*
>
> —Deborah M. Weissman,
> *professor of law,*
> *University of North Carolina*
> *School of Law*

On a typical day in America, as many as three women are murdered by their husbands or intimate partners. While these numbers are indeed shocking, domestic violence and domestic homicide have in fact declined in recent years. Nevertheless, domestic violence remains the leading cause of injury to women. Men also can be victims of such violence, and the children of violent homes often grow up to become victims and/or perpetrators. In addition to the physical and emotional toll of domestic violence, the economic cost to American society also is significant. Domestic violence victims lose nearly 8 million days of paid work per year in the United

States. These realities have led some to fear that the recent statistical drop in domestic violence will lead to complacency. Indeed, some analysts maintain that domestic violence statistics can be deceptive because many abused women and men do not report abuse. In addition, data collected often does not include figures on teen dating violence or violence among unmarried intimate partners. Data on domestic violence in rural areas or on Native American reservations also is scarce. Thus, these advocates argue, more needs to be done to address the problem.

While analysts generally agree that domestic violence is reprehensible, there is wide debate about how society should respond. Some believe that existing criminal laws are adequate to address domestic violence. They argue that expansive government policies and programs are unnecessary and that such policies unconstitutionally interfere with the family. These commentators claim that government-sponsored domestic violence programs often go beyond protecting victims and promote antifamily social philosophies that demonize men. On the other hand, domestic violence activists assert that to address the social causes and consequences of domestic violence, strong government action is necessary. Victims have a right to be protected, they argue, and if local laws and policies are inadequate to do so, the federal government should intervene. Balancing the need to protect family privacy and the often conflicting need to protect people from domestic violence has been an ongoing challenge in the United States. Indeed, these competing values are reflected in the historical debate over how to address domestic violence.

In colonial America, domestic violence was considered a family matter. Women were the property of their husbands, who had the legal right to punish them for disobedience. Colonial courts followed the 1768 English "rule of thumb" law, which stipulated that husbands could beat their wives as long as the stick used was no thicker than the man's thumb. Not until the late nineteenth century did US courts begin to over-turn this right. In 1883, Maryland was the first state to enact a law outlawing wife beating, but it would not be until the mid-twentieth century that the issue would be the subject of public debate. Even then, attitudes about how best to respond to the problem would change little until the end of the century.

During the 1960s, the United States seemed to erupt in violence in the eyes of many. The nation was rocked by race riots, violent antiwar protests, and the assassinations of President John F. Kennedy, his brother Senator Robert F. Kennedy, and civil rights leader the Reverend Martin Luther King Jr. These events prompted the creation of a Presidential Commission on the Causes and Prevention of Violence. The commission's conclusions concerning domestic violence were troubling. As many as 25 percent of men questioned believed it was acceptable, under some circumstances, to hit their spouses. Moreover, the prevailing view was that domestic violence was a family matter and not a crime. When people heard couples fighting, they did not call the police. Most Americans believed that family violence was personal and not their business. Police officers and judges also were reluctant to intervene. It would not be until the late 1970s and into the 1980s that this attitude would change.

In the 1970s, as women began to fight for equal rights, one of the movement's major objectives was to combat domestic violence. Women's rights activists believed that domestic violence was not a family matter but a crime. They argued that women had the right to be free from violence at the hands of their spouses—just as all Americans had the right to be free from violence by strangers. These activists also began to challenge a political and social system that they believed condoned such abuse. Battered women's shelters, hotlines, and grassroots efforts to help women negotiate the legal system began to spring up across the nation. Police officers and judges in some communities also began to change their views. In

1977, Oregon passed the nation's first mandatory-arrest law regarding domestic violence, which required the police to arrest at least one partner when responding to reports of domestic violence. By 1980 all but six states had domestic violence laws. Nevertheless, in many communities, the criminal justice system remained reluctant to approach cases of domestic violence the same way they did other crimes.

Some argue that it took the horrific case of Tracy Thurman, which so shocked the nation, to get attitudes to dramatically shift. Thurman had repeatedly asked the police to help protect her and her son from her estranged husband's abuse. Despite protective orders, the police failed to do so. While at her house, the police refused to intervene while her husband stabbed her thirteen times and broke her neck. A jury in 1984 awarded a $2.3 million judgment against the Torrington, Connecticut, police department for failing to protect Thurman and her son. Thurman's case gained widespread public attention following the television dramatization of her story. Indeed, while some still believed domestic violence to be a private matter, the voices of those who held that victims needed legal protection and that abusers should be prosecuted as criminals began to grow. In fact, Congress passed the Family Violence Prevention and Service Act and the Victims of Crime Act that same year. These laws provided money for states to establish battered women's shelters and hotlines. By the end of the decade, many of the nation's large police departments adopted policies that required officers to make an arrest in domestic violence cases.

Several other widely publicized cases drew public attention to the problem as well. A growing body of evidence also began to dispel the myth that domestic violence was a problem of the poor and uneducated alone. In 1985, President Ronald Reagan forced the resignation of John Fedders, a top Securities and Exchange Commission official, when it was discovered he had for eighteen years repeatedly beaten his wife. In

1987, New York City lawyer Joel Steinberg was convicted of beating to death his eight-year-old adopted daughter Lisa. During his trial, America was introduced to Steinberg's partner, Hedda Nussbaum, whose battered face and unresponsive gaze became the symbol for "battered women's syndrome." Some legal experts argued that this psychological condition, characterized by loss of self-esteem, extreme fear, passivity, and isolation, made it impossible for Nussbaum to intervene and protect Lisa. The case that arguably finally generated the political will to support broad government intervention was the arrest in 1994 of football star and actor O.J. Simpson for the murder of his ex-wife, Nicole Brown Simpson, and her friend, Ronald Goldman. Records showed that Nicole had made frequent calls to police to report her former husband's abuse. Although Simpson was not convicted of the criminal charges, he was found civilly liable for their deaths and was ordered to pay the victims' families compensatory and punitive damages.

Indeed, 1994 was a turning point for what came to be called the domestic violence movement—those who saw domestic violence as a social problem requiring significant government action. That year, Congress passed the Violence Against Women Act (VAWA). In the years since, the act has dedicated billions of dollars to programs that encourage local governments to create coordinated community responses to domestic violence. VAWA also dedicates funds to train police officers and court officials. The act established a national battered women's hotline and made it a federal crime to cross state lines to commit acts of domestic violence. In the 2000 revision of VAWA, Congress added "intimate partners" to the definition of domestic violence to address dating violence and violence against unmarried partners. The 2005 revision dedicated funds to address teen dating violence. By the late 1990s and early into the new millennium, a majority of Americans now saw domestic violence as a serious social problem worthy of government intervention. In fact, studies of social movements suggest that the movement to end domestic violence has so much societal support that a counter movement would be nearly impossible. Nevertheless, there is such a movement—the fathers' rights movement. These activists claim that VAWA unfairly targets men and paints all men as abusers. They argue that VAWA is too broad and criminalizes noncriminal disputes that should remain private, family matters. Although the need to protect victims is strong, privacy remains highly valued in the United States.

The members of the fathers' rights movement do not contest the goal of reducing domestic violence. They oppose the strategy of demonizing men, particularly fathers faced with the dissolution of their families. These activists argue that the domestic violence "industry" uses VAWA programs to help women gain advantage in child custody hearings and to evict men from their homes. They believe that child custody cases should be decided on the facts of the case, not used to promote broad social policies. Public policy professor Jocelyn Elise Crowley summarizes their views. Fathers' rights activists, she maintains, believe that "domestic violence advocates should focus solely on providing services to violence victims, not on pursuing social change by interfering in cases that [do] not specifically involve them."[1] Opponents of broad domestic violence policies also argue that false allegations of abuse are used to gain advantage in divorce proceedings. They maintain that some domestic violence programs encourage women to obtain protective orders, also known as restraining orders. Activists cite cases in which men have been evicted from their homes even when these orders are investigated and dismissed. Moreover, they claim that a protective order is ineffective in preventing violence, "but it is very effective in establishing a firm upper hand in a divorce situation."[2]

Even some in the women's rights movement are shifting their attitudes from the criminal justice approach to protecting victim privacy. Some of the broad policies of VAWA, such as mandatory arrest, actually can limit a woman's autonomy— her ability to make her own choices and deal with family matters in private. According to law professor Kimberly D. Bailey, "Because of the special nature of intimate relationships, some victims may view the violence in their home as a personal matter in the sense that they do not want criminal justice intervention under any circumstances."[3] The goal of the women's and the domestic violence movements was to make the personal political and thus challenge the idea that domestic violence is a private matter. However, by engaging the criminal justice system and the government, these movements may have limited the autonomy of women, as the criminal justice system is a public forum that many women may want to avoid. Policies such as mandatory arrest or pursuing domestic violence cases even when victims choose not to, remove the autonomy that these activists hope to protect. "The limited number of [domestic violence] victims who desire to engage with this system is an important metric in determining the criminal justice system's effectiveness."[4] Thus, in the eyes of some women's rights activists, the criminal justice approach may compete with the very autonomy of the women they hope to protect and, in turn, prevent victims from seeking help. "Unless the desire for privacy is acknowledged and further explored, a significant number of women will continue to be alienated and to suffer from private violence in silence."[5]

Clearly, the competing interests of maintaining personal and family privacy while protecting victims of domestic abuse remains one of the fundamental controversies in the domestic violence debate. *Opposing Viewpoints: Domestic Violence* highlights this tension in many of the viewpoints presented in the following chapters: Is Domestic Violence a Serious Problem? What Are the Causes of Domestic Violence? What Policies Best Address Domestic Violence? and What Laws Will Best Reduce Domestic Violence? From its humble beginnings in the 1960s to the present, the domestic violence movement has done much to protect women, children, and men from violence at the hands of intimate partners. The movement is indeed one of the most powerful social justice movements in American history. Nevertheless, criticism of VAWA spending, the fathers' rights movement, and internal debate among women's rights activists is growing. How policy makers will reconcile these conflicting forces remains to be seen.

Notes

1. Jocelyn Elise Crowley, "Fathers' Rights Groups, Domestic Violence and Political Countermobilization," *Social Forces*, December 2009.
2. Crowley, "Father's Rights Groups."
3. Kimberly D. Bailey, "Lost in Translation," *Journal of Criminal Law and Criminology*, 2010.
4. Bailey, "Lost in Translation."
5. Bailey, "Lost in Translation."

CHAPTER 1

Is Domestic Violence a Serious Problem?

Chapter Preface

"She was 17 when she met her boyfriend, and 20 when she died at his hands," writes *New York Times* reported Elizabeth Olson to describe the death of Heather Norris in Indianapolis, Indiana. Heather tried without success to escape the violent relationship before her boyfriend, Joshua Bean, stabbed her, dismembered her body, and discarded her in trash bags throughout the city in April 2007. Following Heather's death, Indianapolis began a program to train police officers in public schools to recognize the early signs of abuse. Following the stabbing death of Ortralla Mosely, fifteen, and the shooting death of Jennifer Ann Crecente, eighteen, the state of Texas now requires schools to define dating violence in its safety codes. After the murder of Lindsay Ann Burke, Rhode Island today requires schools to teach about dating violence in grades seven through twelve. This hindsight approach frustrates activists who have long claimed that dating violence is a serious problem requiring government-supported programs to educate young people. While not unsympathetic to the families of these murdered girls, others argue that laws already in place address these crimes. Moreover, these analysts believe that the family should be responsible for teaching young people about relationships, not American schools. Indeed the debate over whether dating violence is a problem worthy of government intervention is reflective of similar debates over the seriousness of domestic violence.

Activists did in fact successfully lobby Congress to set aside federal money for educational programs targeting dating violence. Organizations such as the Family Violence Prevention Fund, recently renamed Futures Without Violence, provided testimony before the Senate Judiciary Committee citing studies that as many as one in three adolescent girls in the United States has been a victim of physical, emotional, or verbal abuse from a dating partner. According to Dr. Elizabeth Miller, "Most teens don't understand what a healthy relationship is, often mistaking the controlling behaviors that characterize abuse for signs of love."[2] Moreover, activists maintain, teens who experience dating violence do not have the same options as adults. Shelters often do not accommodate teens, particularly those who are young mothers, although teen mothers are more likely than their peers to experience violence at the hands of their boyfriends. Thus, activists argue, education programs are necessary. "Teens must be taught what is healthy and what is not, and services must be offered to help them through this transition," reasons Juley Fulcher, public policy director at Break the Cycle, an organization that provides information and legal help to young people experiencing domestic violence.

Opponents of funding for education programs to educate young people about healthy relationships do not deny that the deaths of young women at the hands of their dating partners are tragic. They argue, however, that devoting federal funds to support untested educational programs to address dating relationships is both wasteful and beyond the scope of government. Michael McCormick of the American Coalition for Fathers and Children asserts that talking about dating violence "is not in line with public education." He fears that these programs will be less about reducing dating violence and more about perpetuating myths about male socialization that demonize men and support an antifamily, feminist agenda. In truth, teen dating violence statistics show that in high school, boys are as likely to be physically attacked by dating partners as girls. A 2003 study by the Centers for Disease Control and Prevention—conducted in Chicago, Dallas, Milwaukee, San Diego, and Washington, DC—found that 10 percent to 17 percent of girls and 10 percent to 15 percent of boys are abused by their partners. These statistics have led some, including fathers' rights activist David Burroughs of the Safe

Homes for Children and Families Coalition to support dating violence education. "We'd be doing young people a favor by teaching them what healthy relationships are," he maintains. However, he insists that such programs do not perpetuate the myth that only women are victims.

Although Congress did indeed dedicate funds to dating violence education programs, the debate continues. The authors in the following chapter explore these and other issues in answer to the question: Is domestic violence a serious problem? The Violence Against Women Act (VAWA), which funds dating violence education programs, expires in late 2011. The debate over the reauthorization of VAWA and its programs will be heated. Amid the debate, Deborah Norris, Heather's mother, maintains a website to help teens learn to recognize the signs. "Heather always thought she could change people," she explains, "so I guess I'm trying to follow what she wanted."

"*Domestic, or intimate partner, violence may be one of America's most widespread health problems.*"

Domestic Violence Is a Serious Problem

American College of Obstetricians and Gynecologists

In the following viewpoint, the American College of Obstetricians and Gynecologists (ACOG) claims that domestic violence— intentional physical, sexual, or emotional harm inflicted by an intimate partner—is a serious health problem. In fact, the college maintains, approximately 35 percent of women who go to emergency rooms are victims of abuse. What is more, ACOG argues, domestic violence is a significant factor in the abuse of children. If domestic violence victims do not take action to break the cycle of abuse, ACOG asserts, the violence will become more frequent and severe. ACOG, an organization of women's health care providers, promotes ready access to women's health care.

As you read, consider the following questions:

1. According to ACOG, are there any demographic barriers in defining victims of domestic violence?

2. According to the author, what form may domestic abuse take when the victim is pregnant?

3. What does ACOG claim are the three phases of the cycle of abuse?

Domestic, or intimate partner, violence may be one of America's most widespread health problems—and yet one of the least reported. It is of special concern to women because most abuse victims are female.

Domestic violence knows no economic, educational, racial, religious, or age barriers. Abuse happens in intimate relationships between couples from all walks of life. It is most common in couples who are male and female. . . .

What Is Domestic Violence?

Domestic violence is a pattern of threatening or controlling behavior imposed on a woman by someone she loves without regard for her rights, feelings, body, or health. A woman is abused if she has had intentional, often repeated, physical, sexual, or emotional harm done to her by a person with whom she is or has been in an intimate relationship.

Domestic violence affects a woman's health and well-being. About 35% of women who go to emergency rooms are thought to be victims of abuse. More than one-third of female murder victims are killed by their male partners.

Abuse can be actual or threatened. In most violent relationships, mental abuse and "bullying" go along with physical force. Abuse can take any of several forms:

- *Battering and physical assault*—Throwing objects at the victim, pushing, hitting, slapping, kicking, choking, beating, or attacking with a weapon

- *Sexual assault*—Forced sexual activity, including vaginal, oral, or anal intercourse

- *Psychological abuse*—Forcing the victim to perform degrading acts, threatening to harm a partner or her children, attacking or smashing valued objects and pets, or trying to dominate or control a woman's life

There are many ways an abuser may try to control a woman's life. Some may take away her money, food, sleep, clothing, or transportation. Some may keep a woman from being in touch with her family and friends. Others may control her reproductive choices by trying to prevent the use of birth control.

Abuse During Pregnancy

Many pregnant women are abused by their partners. Abuse may begin or increase during pregnancy.

Abuse during pregnancy can pose a risk to both the woman and her fetus. At this time, the abuser is more likely to direct blows at the pregnant woman's breasts and belly. Dangers of this violence include miscarriage, vaginal bleeding, low birth weight, and fetal injury. The fear of harm to her unborn baby often may motivate a woman to leave an abusive relationship.

In other cases, abuse may decrease during pregnancy. In fact, some women feel safe only when they are carrying a child. They know from experience that "he never hits me when I'm pregnant." In these cases, however, abuse may resume shortly after the baby is born. This may lead to repeated pregnancies as a way of escaping abuse.

The Relationship to Child Abuse

Domestic violence may be the most important risk factor for child abuse. In more than one half of the families in which the woman is abused, her children also are abused.

Children who witness family violence or who are abused themselves can be deeply upset by what they see or experi-

What Is Economic Abuse?

- Taking money, credit card or property from a partner without permission

- Racking up debt without the partner's knowledge

- Refusing to supply basics such as food and clothing

- Forbidding a partner from earning money, or being forced by a partner to hand over paychecks

- Monitoring a partner's computer usage

- Harassing a partner at work

Allstate Foundation,
"Crisis: Economics and Domestic Violence" 2009.
www.clicktoempower.org.

ence. The fear, helplessness, and anger children feel in an abusive home often take a major toll. Children may have chronic headaches, stomach problems, or problems with nightmares, sleeping, and bed-wetting. Often, they have difficulty in school. Sometimes, they withdraw from their studies and their friends. Other times, they lash out in anger and get into frequent fights.

Children may come to believe that physical violence is a way of dealing with problems. Female children who are abused are more likely to get into an abusive relationship when they grow up. Male children are more likely to abuse their own partners.

The Abusive Relationship

Because women in abusive relationships are at risk for repeated physical and emotional injury, it is vital to know some of the traits that often characterize the men and women in these relationships. Partners in abusive relationships come from all racial, class, economic, and religious groups from all walks of life.

A male abuser often has a family background of violence and may have low self-esteem and low self-confidence.

However, he may appear to outsiders as a fun-loving, concerned person. He may be very jealous of his partner's relationships with others and blame his partner for his violent acts. Often, he has a problem with alcohol or drugs. This may seem like the cause of the problem, but it is really just an excuse. The abuse seldom stops when alcohol or drug use does.

An abused woman also may have low self-esteem and low self-confidence. Many women believe they somehow cause the abuse and that they can control the abuser by trying to please him or avoid getting him angry. Abusers often tell their partners that they are to blame.

Women stay in abusive relationships for a number of reasons. They often have conflicting feelings—love and loyalty, guilt, and fear of retaliation. They may be financially dependent on their abuser. Whatever her reasons for staying, the daily life of an abused woman is often hectic and scary.

The Cycle of Abuse

Many abused women find themselves caught up in a cycle of abuse that follows a common pattern in many relationships. Unless the woman takes some sort of action to break the cycle, the violence usually becomes more frequent and more severe over time:

- Phase 1—Tension mounts as the abusive partner increases his threats of violence, often calling the woman names or shoving her. During this phase, the abused woman may try to please the abuser or calm him down. Often, her efforts only delay the violence.

- Phase 2—The abuser becomes violent and throws objects at his partner; hits, slaps, kicks, or chokes her; rapes or sexually abuses her; or uses weapons, such as belts, knives, or guns.

- Phase 3—The abuser apologizes and expresses guilt and shame. He promises the violent behavior will not happen again. He often buys his partner gifts. Sometimes the abuser will blame the violence on the woman, saying it would not have happened if she had not said or done something to make him angry.

Overtime, the man tends to put less time and effort into making up. He has learned that his violence is controlling his partner, and he will work less hard at being forgiven or at explaining away his behavior.

> "Given that government authorities define domestic 'violence' as 'name-calling and constant criticizing, insulting, and belittling,' it would appear that many 'reported violent crimes' are not very violent."

The Problem of Domestic Violence Is Exaggerated

Stephen Baskerville

In the following viewpoint, Stephen Baskerville claims that studies exaggerate statistics on domestic violence and child abuse. Studies base these inflated numbers not on actual crimes but on reported allegations, which often prove to be false, he maintains. Indeed, Baskerville argues, divorce lawyers use fabricated or exaggerated allegations of abuse to gain custody of children or marital property for their clients. Unfortunately, feminist rhetoric that convicts falsely accused perpetrators with no evidence trumps due process rights guaranteed by the US Constitution, he reasons. Baskerville, a political scientist, is author of Family Violence in America: The Truth about Domestic Violence and Child Abuse.

Stephen Baskerville, "Innocence Is No Excuse," LewRockwell.com, June 17, 2006. Copyright © 2006 by LewRockwell.com. All rights reserved. Reproduced by permission.

As you read, consider the following questions:

1. In Baskerville's view, why are many "reported violent crimes" not very violent?

2. How does the author translate the claim that alleged abusers have their children kidnapped to intimidate witnesses?

3. According to the author, why are trials, juries, evidence, and the entire apparatus of due process superfluous in domestic violence cases?

The totalitarian mentality of the feminist domestic violence industry was on display recently at the *New York Times*, where two lawyers outline plans for suspending the Bill of Rights. The *Times* normally postures as a champion of civil liberties, but when the malefactors belong to politically unfashionable groups then innocence is no excuse. Only the guilty need constitutional protections, and we may as well just string them up.

A Trumped-Up Issue

"When Words Bear Witness" is a more appropriate headline than Michael Rips and Amy Lester may realize, since their own words reveal the brave new world the feminists and bar associations are creating around the trumped-up issue of "domestic violence."

"Domestic violence accounts for up to 34% of all reported violent crimes," they state. Given that government authorities define domestic "violence" as "name-calling and constant criticizing, insulting, and belittling," it would appear that many "reported violent crimes" are not very violent.

"Reported" crimes are also not proven crimes, and strong incentives exist to report violence where none has taken place. Fabricating abuse accusations ensures custody of children and marital property during divorce. The custody battles are lucrative for lawyers, whose bar associations control judicial appointments and promotions, which is why patently false accusations are treated as fact.

A Perversion of Justice

This perversion of the justice system is now common knowledge among legal practitioners. Thomas Kasper recently described in the *Illinois Bar Journal* how false accusations readily "become part of the gamesmansnip of divorce." Bar associations and even courts themselves sponsor divorce seminars counseling mothers on how to fabricate abuse accusations. "The number of women attending the seminars who smugly—indeed boastfully—announced that they had already sworn out false or grossly exaggerated domestic violence complaints against their hapless husbands, and that the device worked!" astonished Thomas Kiernan, writing in the *New Jersey Law Journal*. "To add amazement to my astonishment, the lawyer-lecturers invariably congratulated the self-confessed miscreants." The *UMKC [University of Missouri-Kansas City] Law Review* reports a survey of judges and attorneys found complaints of disregard for due process and allegations of domestic violence used as a "litigation strategy."

Since most reports involve no crime, it is hardly surprising that domestic violence, as Rips and Lester claim, "is notoriously difficult to prosecute, because [alleged?] victims frequently drop charges or refuse to testify when their [alleged?] abusers [allegedly?] threaten them with further violence." What is this "further violence"? "One study found that many such witnesses received threats that their children would be kidnapped if they testified," says Joan Meier of George Washington University. Their children kidnapped! These wife-beaters are so sophisticated they have organized child kidnapping operations to intimidate witnesses. Translation: The accusations are concocted to separate the children from their fathers, and the fathers understandably want their children back. Each lie necessitates another.

Rips and Lester continue: "In the 1980's and 1990's, the refusal of [alleged?] victims to cooperate in the prosecution of their [alleged?] batterers may have resulted in the dismissal of as many as 70% of all domestic violence cases." The refusal of Rips and Lester to observe the presumption of innocence in their writing is not only standard in feminist literature; it pervades state and federal statutes, including the notorious Violence Against Women Act [VAWA], for which Congress is now [in 2006] considering appropriations. VAWA grants encourage governments to "mandate and encourage police officers to arrest [alleged?] abusers." It is more likely that the cases were dismissed because there was no evidence, because there was no violence and no crime, and because the objective of obtaining custody was accomplished.

Conviction Without Evidence

But now we can secure convictions even when there is no evidence, no victim, and no crime: "Prosecutors, police officers, and advocates for domestic violence victims have developed techniques, together known as 'evidence-based prosecution,' that focus on the use of reliable evidence, like 911 tapes, to build cases that do not depend on the cooperation of the [alleged?] victim." As with the Ministry of Truth,[1] "evidence-based prosecution" is designed to convict those against whom you have no evidence. And since the defendant—excuse me, the "batterer"—can be convicted using hearsay, with no right to face his accuser, it is not really necessary that there even be an accuser, or for that matter a crime.

It is not difficult to see where this is going. In Britain, "special domestic violence courts" allow third parties such as civil servants and pressure groups to use "relaxed rules of evi-

1. The Ministry of Truth refers to one of four ministries that govern George Orwell's fictional Oceania in his novel *Nineteen Eighty-Four*. The name is a misnomer—the ministry's purpose is to create falsehoods passed off as truths.

dence and the lower burden of proof" to bring actions against those they identify as batterers, even if no alleged "victim" comes forward (or even exists). "Victim support groups," who say women "should be spared having to take legal action," can now act in the name of an anonymous or purported plaintiff to seize the children, homes, and other property of men who have not been convicted of any crime. Similar "domestic violence courts" are being created in the United States and Canada, where "conviction rates have risen" and "guilty pleas are way up," *Mother Jones* magazine enthuses. In other words, rigged trials and the certainty of conviction allow prosecutors to extort guilty pleas.

Suspending Due Process

Sending men to jail is apparently now a virtue in itself. In San Diego, Rips and Lester report with glee, suspending due process protections "obtains convictions in about 88% of its cases." Convicting people of crimes—thousands of people of whose guilt or innocence we can have no first-hand knowledge—is now something to be celebrated for its own sake.

Guilt used to be determined by juries weighing evidence in specific cases. But Rips and Lester apparently know that these "batterers" are guilty *en masse*, and all that remains is removing constitutional impediments to convicting them. Trials, juries, evidence, and the entire apparatus of due process are superfluous because guilt is not defined by whether an individual committed a specific deed. Guilt is a foregone conclusion because the defendant belongs to a class that is guilty by political definition. The New Jersey family court invokes feminist jargon to argue that allowing due process protections to abuse defendants "perpetuates the cycle of power and control whereby the [alleged?] perpetrator remains the one with the power and the [alleged?] victim remains powerless."

My niggling interpolations are no doubt annoying for prosecutors whose careers depend on their conviction rates.

They have effectively institutionalized the archetypal loaded question, "When did you stop beating your wife?"

"A 2007 survey ... of young adults found that 71 percent of the instigators in nonreciprocal partner violence were women."

Domestic Violence Against Men Is a Serious Problem

Mark Mahnkey

In the following viewpoint, Mark Mahnkey argues that women are as likely to abuse their partners as are men. Studies show that men experience 38 percent of domestic violence injuries but are reluctant to report incidents, he maintains. Because these incidents go unreported, the media paints a one-sided picture of domestic violence, Mahnkey asserts. Reporting misleading statistics only makes the problem worse, he reasons, because women abusers and their male victims do not get the services they need. Mahnkey is director of public policy for the State of Washington Civil Rights Council.

As you read, consider the following questions:

1. What are some of the studies that Mahnkey cites to support his claim that women are as violent as their male partners?

2. According to the author, what is the impact of aggressive domestic violence laws?

3. In the author's view, what should the domestic violence industry do if it really wanted to prevent harm?

October is Domestic Violence [DV] Awareness Month. The month is designed to increase awareness of how to make our homes safe from partner violence. So what is the truth about intimate partner aggression? Nearly 200 scientific studies point to one simple conclusion: Women are at least as likely as men to engage in partner aggression.

Irene Hanson Frieze, in *Psychology of Women's Quarterly*, says "Research indicates that women can be just as violent as their partners." Don Dutton from the University of British Columbia notes that "Recent evidence from the best designed studies indicates that intimate partner violence is committed by both genders with often equal consequences." And the *Journal of Family Psychology* in 2006 tells us that "Differences were observed in the rates of male and female partner violence, with female violence occurring more frequently."

A 2007 survey sponsored by the U.S. Centers for Disease Control of young adults found that 71 percent of the instigators in nonreciprocal partner violence were women. A national survey of married and co-habiting partners found that 8 percent of women engaged in severe partner violence, while only 4 percent of men were involved in severe violence.

Unexpected Results

The result of this recent peer-reviewed and published research is much different than you have been led to believe, but you are not alone. Many researchers have noted lately that the results of their research are much different than they expected.

Men often suffer injuries from their wives or girlfriends. According to a 2000 analysis by John Archer, men suffer 38 percent of all injuries arising from partner aggression. But men often endure their pain in silence and don't report the incident. As a result, the media and others often present a one-sided and distorted view of the problem.

Domestic violence industry advocates often make claims such as "95 percent of DV victims are women." These false statements only make the problem worse because:

- Abusive women can't get the help they need.

- Male victims are denied services.

- False allegations of abuse escalate partner conflict and families are harmed.

- Aggressive domestic violence laws short-circuit due process and create a presumption of "guilty until proven innocent."

The Problem of Violence Against Men

Recall two recent incidents to illustrate the problem.

One evening Warren Moon, then a National Football League quarterback, got into a fight with his wife. Police were called and Mr. Moon was arrested. Against Mrs. Moon's wishes, the case went to trial. Placed on the witness stand, Mrs. Moon admitted that she was the one who had started the fight by throwing a candlestick, and that her husband had only acted in self-defense. Warren Moon was acquitted.

A judge in New Mexico granted a restraining order against David Letterman for sending messages over the television to a woman in that state. The judge was quoted as saying "if they fill out the paperwork correctly, I always grant the restraining order."

Prosecuting False Accusers

If the domestic violence industry really wanted to prevent harm, they would support legislation to prosecute false accusers, and attempt to help all victims, both male and female.

"Say No to Domestic Violence," cartoon by Gustavo Rodriguez. www.cartoonstock.com.

While they claim to offer service to men, that service is primarily offering "treatment" courses, which are majorly ineffective. These courses have no objective criteria for completion, other than requiring a statement that the dispute was exclusively the alleged perpetrator's fault, with not an iota of responsibility or accountability on the part of the "victim," disregarding the research that shows most intimate partner violence to be mutual. There is a continuing, solid resistance to making all restraining orders mutual, even though that would greatly decrease the chances of the parties interacting and make both parties accountable for their behavior. Lastly, they would encourage prosecution of false accusers, allowing the real victims the attention and services they need.

The domestic violence industry often complains about "blaming the victim," but in the face of the new research and evidence, they now not only continue to blame the half of the victims that are male, but to incarcerate him as well.

Thirty-some years ago, there was a thankfully successful campaign to get rape of females taken seriously. Now is the time to get violence against men by female partners taken seriously.

| "Intimate partner violence continues to largely, overwhelmingly, be perpetrated by men against women."

Domestic Violence Against Women Is More Common than Domestic Violence Against Men

Elsie Hambrook

In the following viewpoint, Elsie Hambrook argues that women are more likely to be victims of domestic violence than are men. In fact, of Canadian murder victims killed by a current or former spouse, 38 percent are women and only 4 percent are men, she claims. Men are indeed victims of violence but usually at the hands of other men, Hambrook asserts. Claims that men sometimes are victims of women abusers minimizes the seriousness of a problem that is faced primarily by women, she reasons. Hambrook, chair of the Canadian New Brunswick Advisory Council on the Status of Women, writes for the Moncton, New Brunswick, Times & Transcript.

As you read, consider the following questions:

1. What happens when the definition of domestic violence is expanded to include violence against children, in Hambrook's view?

2. According to the author, what is the purpose of "What about the Men?" comments?

3. Who suffers when women are victims of violence, according to the author?

"I'll tell you one area where women are equal: as perpetrators of domestic violence."

This comment, made online in response to one of my recent columns, can be heard or read on a regular basis in various forms. Some commenters even suggest, for instance, that the women's movement suppresses evidence that women are as violent, or more violent, than men.

Men are absolutely frequent victims of violence. Men are the victims of violence more often than women. Usually it is at the hands of other men.

You can look it up.

Looking at the Facts

There are men who suffer abuse at the hands of their female partners—and it is unacceptable. That is not a typical scenario. Intimate partner violence continues to largely, overwhelmingly, be perpetrated by men against women.

It is women who are most likely to be forced to leave their homes and communities to escape violence while abusive men stay in the home.

This is a fact.

Women are much more likely than men to be raped by their intimate partners.

That's irrefutable.

Women are more likely than men to be victims of domestic homicide.

Count the bodies.

Of all Canadian female murder victims, 38 per cent are killed by their current or former spouse. Of all male murder victims, four per cent are killed by their current or former spouse. Last year [in 2010], there were 2,000 reports, that the police ruled were founded, of a female victim of violence at the hands of a current or former partner in the province, more than double the number from five years ago.

If we expand the definition of domestic violence to include violence against children: the perpetrator is male in 69 per cent of cases of a child who is physically assaulted by a family member; it is the mother in 27 per cent of these cases. When a child is sexually abused by a family member, it's a male relative in 97 per cent of cases.

I don't bring up these points to minimize male victims of partner violence. I make these points because these are the facts and if we are to address partner violence effectively, we have to acknowledge them and the gendered nature of this violence. We can't pretend that partner violence victimizes everyone equally. And we can't ignore that women's unequal status in society adds to women's vulnerability and to abuse victims' difficulties.

Changing the Conversation

Comments about women's violence are an effort to change the conversation. Commenters want to change the subject to "What About the Men?!"

"What About the Men?!" is a phrase that you'll find floating around blogs and conversations, when someone is trying to shift—or end—a discussion that irritates them. In Canada, "What About the Men?!" also manifests itself in the form of "Why isn't there a Status of Men?!"

Family Violence Statistics

The majority (73%) of family violence victims were female [according to a 2005 report]. Females were 84% of spouse abuse victims and 86% of victims of abuse at the hands of a boyfriend or girlfriend.

While about three-fourths of the victims of family violence were female, about three-fourths of the persons who committed family violence were male. . . .

Females were 58% of family murder victims. Of all the murders of females in 2002, family members were responsible for 43%. . . .

Eight in ten murderers who killed a family member were male. Males were 83% of spouse murderers and 75% of murderers who killed a boyfriend or girlfriend.

Bureau of Justice Statistics, June 2005.
www.ojp.usdoj.gov.

The question about men's reality can be posed in good faith and productively. More about that later.

But "What About the Men?!" comments are rarely made in good faith. They are rarely made in an effort to add to a meaningful discussion. These comments are more often hostile and meant to grind the conversation to a halt. It is meant to take away from the few occasions where women's concerns are taken seriously.

The comment, "I'll tell you one area where women are equal: as perpetrators of domestic violence" is a good example of this tactic. It tells a falsehood to derail the conversation.

The legitimate question that could be raised surrounding intimate partner violence is "what about the rigid gender role that many abusive men find themselves in?"

What about the frustration, despair and depression that come from living in strict stereotyped roles? The role prescribed for boys and men—boys are tough, men are in charge—must be challenged.

Many other cases where the question about the men was asked sincerely and productively, are as a result of gender-based analysis being done by an organization or a government.

Recently the National Institute of Mental Health in the United States tested various approaches to address the problem of men under-using mental health services. They had developed a gender neutral publication, but men did not seem to respond any better to the offer of services.

Then a "male-sensitive" brochure was developed, aimed at improving attitudes about seeking counseling. It worked with depressive men to a greater degree than other brochures.

It was the only brochure that significantly reduced self-stigma, where you perceive yourself as weak if you seek help. The depression symptoms they described were those that men might have: men may mask depression with externalizing behaviours such as workaholism, substance use, aggression, recklessness, withdrawal.

They used language more acceptable for men ("mental health consultant" instead of "therapist") and described counseling as a cost-effective, client-directed team effort. They countered the idea that depression is the product of a weak will by citing the biological bases of depression.

Women's gains are not men's loss.

Most people, including most men, understand that and also suffer when the women they love around them are victims of violence and discrimination.

This is not a competition. Even if women were as violent as men, we'd still have a violence problem.

| "For one in 10 teens, abuse is a very
real part of dating relationships."

Teen Dating Violence
Is a Serious Problem

Carrie Mulford and Peggy C. Giordano

In the following viewpoint, Carrie Mulford and Peggy C. Giordano assert that teen dating violence is a serious problem that differs from adult domestic violence. In fact, they argue, applying the adult perspective may account for the split among experts about the nature of the problem. For example, the authors claim, power relationships among teens are different; thus abuse in teen relationships is often mutual. In addition, they maintain, because teens lack relationship experience as well as communication skills, conflicts can lead to verbal and physical aggression. Mulford is an analyst with the National Institute of Justice; Giordano is a professor of sociology at Bowling Green State University in Ohio.

As you read, consider the following questions:

1. According to Mulford and Giordano, why is the phenomenon of teen dating violence not fully understood?

2. In the authors' opinion, how do peers influence teen dating violence?

3. What do the authors claim are the implications of the differences between adult and teen relationships on teen dating violence prevention and intervention strategies?

Most teenagers do not experience physical aggression when they date. However, for one in 10 teens, abuse is a very real part of dating relationships.

According to the 2007 Youth Risk Behavior Survey, approximately 10 percent of adolescents nationwide reported being the victim of physical violence at the hands of a romantic partner during the previous year. The rate of psychological victimization is even higher: Between two and three in 10 reported being verbally or psychologically abused in the previous year, according to the National Longitudinal Study of Adolescent Health.

As for perpetration rates, there are currently no nationwide estimates for who does the abusing, and state estimates vary significantly. In South Carolina, for example, nearly 8 percent of adolescents reported being physically violent to a romantic partner. Interestingly, the rates of reported victimization versus perpetration in the state were similar for boys and girls. However, when it comes to severe teen dating violence—including sexual and physical assault—girls were disproportionately the victims.

Findings at Odds with Experience

At a recent workshop on teen dating violence, co-sponsored by the U.S. Departments of Justice (DOJ) and Health and Human Services (HHS), researchers presented findings from several studies that found that girls and boys perpetrate the same frequency of physical aggression in romantic relationships. This finding was at odds with what practitioners attending the workshop said they encounter in their professional experience.

Most of the practitioners in attendance—representing national organizations, schools and victim service community-based agencies—said that they primarily see female victims, and when they discuss teen dating violence with students, they hear that boys are the primary perpetrators.

So what *is* the reality?

Because teen dating violence has only recently been recognized as a significant public health problem, the complex nature of this phenomenon is not fully understood. Although research on rates of perpetration and victimization exists, research that examines the problem from a longitudinal perspective and considers the dynamics of teen romantic relationships is lacking. Consequently, those in the field have to rely on an *adult* framework to examine the problem of teen dating violence.

However, we find that this adult framework does not take into account key differences between adolescent and adult romantic relationships. And so, to help further the discussion, we offer in this [viewpoint] a gender-based analysis of teen dating violence with a developmental perspective. We look at what we know—and what we don't know—about who is the perpetrator and who is the victim in teen dating violence. We also discuss how adult and adolescent romantic relationships differ in the hope that an examination of existing research will help us better understand the problem and move the field toward the creation of developmentally appropriate prevention programs and effective interventions for teenagers.

What the Research Says

In 2001–2005, Peggy Giordano and her colleagues at Bowling Green State University interviewed more than 1,300 seventh, ninth and 11th graders in Toledo, Ohio. More than half of the girls in physically aggressive relationships said both they and their dating partner committed aggressive acts during the relationship. About a third of the girls said they were the sole perpetrators, and 13 percent reported that they were the sole victims. Almost half of the boys in physically aggressive relationships reported mutual aggression, nearly half reported they were the sole victim, and 6 percent reported that they were the sole perpetrator.

These findings are generally consistent with another study that looked at more than 1,200 Long Island, N.Y., high school students who were currently dating. In that 2007 survey, 66 percent of boys and 65 percent of girls who were involved in physically aggressive relationships reported mutual aggression. Twenty-eight percent of the girls said that they were the sole perpetrator; 5 percent said they were the sole victim. These numbers were reversed for the boys: 5 percent said they were the sole perpetrator; 27 percent the sole victim.

In a third study, teen couples were videotaped while performing a problem-solving task. Researchers later reviewed the tapes and identified acts of physical aggression that occurred between the boys and girls during the exercise. They found that 30 percent of all the participating couples demonstrated physical aggression by both partners. In 17 percent of the participating couples, only the girls perpetrated physical aggression, and in 4 percent, only the boys were perpetrators. The findings suggest that boys are less likely to be physically aggressive with a girl when someone else can observe their behavior.

Considered together, the findings from these three studies reveal that frequently there is mutual physical aggression by girls and boys in romantic relationships. However, when it comes to *motivations* for using violence and the consequences of being a victim of teen dating violence, the differences between the sexes are pronounced. Although both boys and girls report that anger is the primary motivating factor for using violence, girls also commonly report self-defense as a motivating factor, and boys also commonly cite the need to exert control. Boys are also more likely to react with laughter when their partner is physically aggressive. Girls experiencing teen dating violence are more likely than boys to suffer long-term negative behavioral and health consequences, including suicide attempts, depression, cigarette smoking and marijuana use.

Applying Adult Perspectives

Why do teenagers commit violence against each other in romantic relationships? We have already touched on the existing body of research on perpetration and victimization rates. Yet there is not a great deal of research that uses a longitudinal perspective or that considers the dynamics of teen romantic relationships. As a result, practitioners and researchers in the field tend to apply an adult intimate partner violence framework when examining the problem of teen dating violence.

A split currently exists, however, among experts in the adult intimate partner violence arena, and attendees at the DOJ-HHS teen dating workshop mirrored this divide.

Some experts hold that men and women are mutually combative and that this behavior should be seen as part of a larger pattern of family conflict. Supporters of this view generally cite studies that use "act" scales, which measure the number of times a person perpetrates or experiences certain acts, such as pushing, slapping or hitting. These studies tend to show that women report perpetrating slightly more physical violence than men. It is interesting to note that most studies on teen dating violence that have been conducted to date have relied primarily on "act" scales.

Another group of experts holds that men generally perpetrate serious intimate partner violence against women. They contend that men in patriarchal societies use violence to exert and maintain power and control over women. These experts also maintain that "act" scales do not accurately reflect the nature of violence in intimate relationships because they do not consider the degree of injury inflicted, coercive and controlling behaviors, the fear induced, or the context in which the acts occurred. Studies using "act" scales, they contend, lack information on power and control and emphasize the more common and relatively minor forms of aggression rather than more severe, relatively rare forms of violence in dating and intimate partner relationships. Instead, supporters of this perspective use data on injuries and in-depth interviews with victims and perpetrators.

We believe, however, that applying either of these adult perspectives to adolescents is problematic. Although both views of adult intimate partner violence can help inform our understanding of teen dating violence, it is important to consider how adolescent romantic relationships differ from adult romantic relationships in several key areas.

How Teen Dating Violence Differs

One difference between adolescent and adult relationships is the absence of elements traditionally associated with greater male power in adult relationships. Adolescent girls are not typically dependent on romantic partners for financial stability, and they are less likely to have children to provide for and protect.

The study of seventh, ninth and 11th graders in Toledo, for example, found that a majority of the boys and girls who were interviewed said they had a relatively "equal say" in their romantic relationships. In cases in which there was a power imbalance, they were more likely to say that the female had more power in the relationship. Overall, the study found that the boys perceived that they had less power in the relationship than the girls did. Interestingly, males involved in relationships in which one or both partners reported physical aggression had a perception of less power than males in relationships without physical aggression. Meanwhile, the girls reported no perceived difference in power regardless of whether their relationships included physical aggression.

Who Perpetrates Teen Dating Violence?

How girls in physically aggressive relationships see it

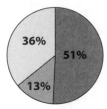

Toledo Adolescent Relationship Study

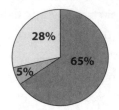

Suffolk County Study of Dating
Aggression in High Schools

How boys in physically aggressive relationships see it

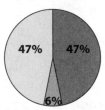

Toledo Adolescent Relationship Study

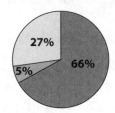

Suffolk County Study of Dating
Aggression in High Schools

What is observed in physically aggressive couples

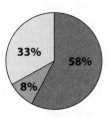

Oregon Youth (Couples) Study

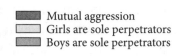

Mutual aggression
Girls are sole perpetrators
Boys are sole perpetrators

TAKEN FROM: Carrie Mulford and Peggy C. Giordano, "Teen Dating Violence," *NIJ Journal*, October 2008.

It is interesting to note that adults who perpetrate violence against family members often see themselves as powerless in their relationships. This dynamic has yet to be adequately explored among teen dating partners.

A Lack of Relationship Experience

A second key factor that distinguishes violence in adult relationships from violence in adolescent relationships is the lack of experience teens have in negotiating romantic relationships. Inexperience in communicating and relating to a romantic partner may lead to the use of poor coping strategies, including verbal and physical aggression. A teen who has difficulty expressing himself or herself may turn to aggressive behaviors (sometimes in play) to show affection, frustration or jealousy. A recent study in which boys and girls participated in focus groups on dating found that physical aggression sometimes stemmed from an inability to communicate feelings and a lack of constructive ways to deal with frustration.

As adolescents develop into young adults, they become more realistic and less idealistic about romantic relationships. They have a greater capacity for closeness and intimacy. Holding idealistic beliefs about romantic relationships can lead to disillusionment and ineffective coping mechanisms when conflict emerges. It also seems reasonable to expect that physical aggression may be more common when adolescents have not fully developed their capacity for intimacy, including their ability to communicate.

The Influence of Peers

We would be remiss to try to understand teen behavior and not consider the profound influence of friends. Peers exert more influence on each other during their adolescent years than at any other time. Research has confirmed that peer attitudes and behaviors are critical influences on teens' attitudes and behaviors related to dating violence.

Not only are friends more influential in adolescence than in adulthood, but they are also more likely to be "on the scene" and a key element in a couple's social life. In fact, roughly half of adolescent dating violence occurs when a third party is present. Relationship dynamics often play out in a very public way because teens spend a large portion of their time in school and in groups. For various reasons, a boyfriend or girlfriend may act very differently when in the presence of peers, a behavior viewed by adolescents as characteristic of an unhealthy relationship. For example, boys in one focus group study said that if a girl hit them in front of their friends, they would need to hit her back to "save face."

Conflict over how much time is spent with each other versus with friends, jealousies stemming from too much time spent with a friend of the opposite sex, and new romantic possibilities are all part of the social fabric of adolescence. Although "normal" from a developmental perspective, navigating such issues can cause conflict and, for some adolescents, lead to aggressive responses and problematic coping strategies, such as stalking, psychological or verbal abuse, and efforts to gain control.

Where Do We Go from Here?

Adult relationships differ substantially from adolescent dating in their power dynamics, social skill development and peer influence. These factors are critical to understanding physical violence and psychological abuse in early romantic relationships and may help explain the similar perpetration rates among boys and girls suggested by current statistics.

All of this points to important implications for teen dating violence prevention and intervention strategies. Because girls engage in high levels of physical aggression and psychological abuse and most abusive relationships are characterized by mutual aggression, prevention efforts must be directed toward both males and females, and interventions for victims should include services and programming for boys and girls. Interventions must also distinguish between severe forms of violence that produce injury and fear and other more common abuse, and they must respond with appropriate safety planning, mental health services, and criminal or juvenile justice involvement.

More research on traditionally gendered relationship dynamics—and the links to relationship violence—is also needed. For instance, some male behavior may stem from an attempt to emulate other males who they believe (not always accurately, as data show) are confident and "in charge." Further, nearly one in five adolescent girls reports having sex with a partner three or more years older. These girls are at increased risk of acquiring a sexually transmitted disease because they are less likely to use a condom—possibly a result of unequal power dynamics in these relationships. This power imbalance might also increase their risk for violent victimization by older partners.

And finally, research on the extent to which teens involved in abusive relationships become involved in adult abusive relationships—whether as victims or perpetrators—is sorely needed. Many delinquent youth, for example, have a well-documented path of illegal behavior; this behavior peaks in adolescence and dramatically declines in early adulthood. A similar look at aggressive adolescent romantic relationships may help us better understand the possible progression from teen dating violence to adult intimate partner violence.

| "Dating violence is not increasing or
'epidemic' among high school students."

The Problem of Teen Dating Violence Is Exaggerated

Mike Males

In the following viewpoint, Mike Males argues that teen dating violence is not on the rise. In fact, he claims, surveys show quite the opposite. Nevertheless, organizations use exaggeration techniques to market their dating abuse programs, Males maintains. For example, he asserts, program advocates include in their survey results answers to speculative questions and expand the definition to include such things as being told how to dress. Such exaggerations, Males reasons, teach teens that normal disagreements amount to abuse and downplay the violence and sexual abuse that may occur at home. Males, senior researcher at the Center on Juvenile and Criminal Justice, is author of The Scapegoat Generation: America's War on Adolescents.

As you read, consider the following questions:

1. According to Males, what do recent studies such as the Youth Behavior Risk Survey reveal about teen dating abuse?

2. What example does the author provide of the exaggeration technique of citing one-time behaviors?

3. In the author's view, how do program advocates obscure important causes of teen dating abuse?

American secondary schools are coming under intense pressure from corporations, politicians, and the news media to implement prescribed "teenage dating abuse" programs. A recent [2008] resolution by the National Association of Attorneys General [NAAG] urged "school districts to incorporate dating violence education into health education curriculums in middle and or high school." "We are committed to addressing this issue through education," declared Rhode Island Attorney General Patrick Lynch, the resolution's chief sponsor. "A curriculum such as Liz Claiborne Inc.'s Love Is Not Abuse is an effective way to begin the process of education, prevent abuse and help to save lives."

Conflicting Numbers

But is teen dating abuse "increasing" to "staggering" levels, as program advocates insist, justifying entire new school curriculums to combat it? Commonly cited numbers reported in the press and by program advocates, summarized by the American Bar Association's Teen Dating Violence Initiative, indeed appear alarming. "A comparison of Intimate Partner Violence rates between teens and adults reveals that teens are at higher risk of intimate partner abuse. . . . Approximately 1 in 5 female high school students report being physically and/or sexually abused by a dating partner." "Females ages 16–24 are more vulnerable to intimate partner violence than any other age group—at a rate almost triple the national average."

However, the most alarming numbers being cited reflect 1990s data. More recent numbers from larger surveys are considerably lower. In 2003, the Youth Behavior Risk Survey found 9% of students in grades 9–12 reported having a dating partner "hit, slap, or physically hurt you on purpose" at least once. In 2005, the Bureau of Justice Statistics' Intimate Partner Violence report found that 2.1% of students ages 12–19 (including 0.9% of youths age 12–15, and 3.4% of those age 16–19) experienced any form of physical violence (murder, simple assault, aggravated assault, rape, robbery, or sexual assault) from an intimate partner (a spouse, ex-spouse, boyfriend/girlfriend, ex-boyfriend/girlfriend, same-sex partner). This report relied on the National Crime Victimization Survey [NCVS], America's largest, most consistent, and only long-term measure of such crime, with samples of more than 70,000 Americans every year since 1993.

A 2008 survey commissioned by Liz Claiborne, Inc., a fashion corporation that markets dating abuse programs, found similar levels for younger students. Its survey of 1,043 students age 11–14 found that 2% of 11–14 year-olds (14 males and 7 females) reported ever having had a partner "hit, slap, punch, choke, or kick" them and 1% reported having been pressured into sexual activity (five males and eight females; whether these duplicated some of those physically abused is not shown).

Declining, Not Rising Dating Abuse Rates

Recent surveys do not find teens uniquely at risk. The Intimate Partner Violence survey finds that in the most recent five years, 2001–05, teens age 16–19 had lower rates of intimate-partner violence (3.4%) than adults age 20–24 (6.5%) and 25–34 (4.7%) and somewhat above adults age 35–49 (2.8%), while 12–15-year-olds experienced the lowest levels of dating violence (0.9%) of any age except 65 and older (less than 0.1%). Given that intimate partner violence rises sharply as socioeconomic status falls and that teenagers and young adults suffer considerably higher rates of poverty and socioeconomic disadvantage than older adults, teens appear to experience fairly low rates of intimate partner violence for their demographics.

Nor is dating abuse rising. The long-term measures available such as FBI Uniform Crime Reports, Monitoring the Future, and the National Crime Victimization Survey variously agree that murder, rape, robbery, assault, sexual assault, and kidnapping involving both younger and older teens has dropped dramatically over the last 10 to 20 years, most to all time lows. Intimate partner violence has fallen the most dramatically. The NCVS found that from 1993 to 2005, the proportion of teenage females reporting intimate partner violence fell by 70%.

These seemingly calming trends and numbers have not moderated program advocates' alarms, however. "One in three teens reports knowing a friend or peer who has been hit, punched, kicked, slapped or physically hurt by their dating partner," a representative of Liz Claiborne stated. "The number of tweens [ages 11 to 12] in abusive relationships (is) staggering." NAAG's 2008 resolution agreed: "Teen dating violence has become a prevalent problem in high schools, junior high schools and middle schools throughout our country.... Recent studies have shown that teen dating violence is starting" as young as ages "11 to 14."

Using Exaggerration Techniques

Investigation reveals that program advocates have used several questionable techniques with troubling implications for responsible programming to drastically exaggerate the prevalence of teen dating abuse. In particular, advocates have extended the definition of "teen dating violence" far beyond NAAG's criterion of "a pattern of controlling and abusive behavior of one person over another within a romantic relationship including verbal, emotional, physical, sexual and financial abuse."

Program advocates' first exaggeration technique, aside from including figures for 20–24-year-olds (an age group with considerably higher violence rates) as "teenage dating violence" and continuing to repeat higher 1990s numbers, is to cite one-time behaviors rather than those documenting a "pattern of controlling and abusive behavior." As will be seen, a girl saying something to make the boy sitting next to her in class feel bad about himself could constitute "dating abuse" by Liz Claiborne's definition.

The second exaggeration technique is to emphasize not the small numbers of teens who report actually being abused, but secondhand guesses by teens in response to speculative questions as to whether "people your age" might suffer abuse by dating partners. Thus, while 2% of 11–14-year-olds reported being abused, 20% speculated that undefined peers might experience dating abuse. Of course, guesses about what others "your age" are experiencing can be inflated by one case known to many students, gossip, rumors, and media reports.

Expanding Definitions

Program advocates' third and most disturbing exaggeration technique is to expand the definitions of "relationship" and "abuse" substantially beyond behaviors normally associated with the terms. In Claiborne's survey, a "relationship" includes not just regular dating, but "sitting next to each other in school," "admitting that he/she likes the other person," "flirting," and "calling or texting each other regularly." "Abuse" includes partners who "made you feel bad or embarrassed about yourself," "made you feel nervous about doing something he/she doesn't like," "hurt you with words," or "tried to tell you how to dress"—even once.

Finally, the most alarming dating abuse numbers come from tiny subsamples of teens, not the whole sample. For example, consider Claiborne's statement, "69% of all teens who had sex by age 14 said they have gone through one or more types of abuse in a relationship." Having "sex" referred to not just intercourse or oral sex, but ever "having gone further than kissing and making out." "Abuse," as noted, was defined to include just about any problem. Thus, the "69%" figure actually referred to around 30 of the 1,043 youths surveyed who had experienced even the mildest negative interaction with a partner with whom they had gone further than kissing or making out.

Claiborne's survey found the percentages of teens suffering verbal and emotional abuse, violent threats, and extreme jealousy from a dating or "hookup" partner rare as well. Just 8% had a partner who ever (even once) "asked you to only spend time with him/her," "called you names or put you down" (7%), "hurt you with words" (6%), or "threatened to spread rumors about you" (4%). For behaviors more commonly considered emotionally abusive and controlling, just 3% of teens had "been concerned about your safety (being hurt physically because of him/her)" and 2% reported that a dating or hookup partner actually had "threatened to hurt you or himself/herself if you were to break up."

Nor does the survey confirm Claiborne's and news media assertions that modern communications technology has opened up vast new theaters of meanness. Only 2% of 11–12-year-olds and 7% of 13–14-year-olds had ever had a partner say anything "really mean" about them using cellphones, text messages, instant messaging, social sites, blogs, or other Internet tools one or more times.

Implementing Unnecessary Programs

If program advocates' own recent survey is credible, then, the large majority of teens have never experienced the controlling behavior or physical, sexual, verbal, or emotional violence characteristic of dating abuse even once, let alone as a pattern of mistreatment. Abuses appear to be rare and dropping, not epidemic and rising. Around one in 50 younger teens and one in 30 older teens report intimate partner violence in a year's time, levels similar to those among adults.

Should schools adopt prescribed dating abuse programs, then? Aside from the budget and time-on-task issues entailed in adding full-scale dating abuse programs to already overloaded high school curriculums amid funding cutbacks, the deceptions advocates have used to market these programs present troubling indicators of potentially harmful biases underlying these curriculums.

First, the extreme exaggerations marketers employ lend the impression that violence is normative to teen relationships. They stereotype even very young students as promiscuous, violent, and cruel. Such negative stereotypes toward young people do not connote the attitude of respect programs should seek to inculcate.

Second, program advocates' overbroad definitions risk teaching students the unrealistic lesson that normal, occasional disagreements and unharmonious feelings constitute "abuse" and that healthy relationships must always be blissful. Even the soundest adult marriages would be rated as abusive according to Claiborne's definitions.

Ignoring Real Causes

Finally, by ignoring or downplaying uncomfortable precursors such as parental, household, and community violence in favor of more comfortable, superficial explanations, programs obscure important causes. For example, Claiborne representatives blame tweens' "early sexual experimentation" as the cause of "increased levels of teen dating violence and abuse." However, aside from strong evidence that both teenage and adult "intimate partner violence has been declining," a solid body of research indicates that growing up in violent homes and suffering childhood violence and sexual abuse, usually inflicted by parents or caretakers, is the most reliable predictor both of early sexual activity, violence, and abuse. The latest Child Maltreatment report substantiated 200,000 violent and sexual abuses and 100,000 emotional abuses inflicted on children and youths by parents in 2006.

Dating violence is not increasing or "epidemic" among high school students but does affect a fraction. It does not appear to be a distinct form of violence, but part of a continuum that includes abusive parents and violent homes and communities. This indicates that for most schools, targeted referral and counseling training, services, and curriculums that include dating violence as one type of health risk, rather than full-scale programs dedicated solely to dating violence, represent the most viable educational approach. Whatever strategies are adopted in violence prevention education, the most accurate information rather than unwarranted exaggerations and a respectful approach toward young people rather than negative stereotypes are required.

"One out of every three women world-wide is physically, sexually or otherwise abused during her lifetime."

Domestic Violence Is a Global Problem

Humaira Shahid and Ritu Sharma

In the following viewpoint, Humaira Shahid and Ritu Sharma claim that one of every three of the world's women suffers from some sort of abuse. However, legal reforms and programs that empower women are gaining support, they assert. Indeed, Shahid and Sharma argue, many Americans believe that ending violence against women worldwide should be a priority. Programs that empower women economically and provide them with access to justice will help promote societies that are less violent and more just, they conclude. Shahid, a former Pakistani legislator, conducts research at the Radcliffe Institute for Advanced Study at Harvard University. Sharma is cofounder and president of Women Thrive Worldwide, an organization based in Washington, DC.

As you read, consider the following questions:

1. According to the viewpoint, what customary practices were abolished in Pakistan in 2003?

2. What issues are addressed by the International Violence Against Women Act, according to the authors?

3. What examples do the authors cite of women's accomplishments despite the odds?

Eight Years ago [2002], Nasreen (not her real name) walked into the office of the *Daily Khabrain* newspaper in Lahore, Pakistan, and demanded justice. She stripped off her clothes, revealing a black and blue body covered with wounds and cigarette burns. She'd been gang raped. With tears in her eyes, she said, "My husband hired three men and got me raped in front of him because I was tired of his abuse and demanded the divorce that Islam gave me a right to. He didn't even respect me as the mother of his children. . . . I just want justice in the name of God."

Nasreen was just one of millions of women who suffer acid attacks, rape, forced marriages and other unimaginable forms of violence around the world. One out of every three women worldwide is physically, sexually or otherwise abused during her lifetime. The good news is that there are thousands of organizations in communities around the world for abused women. These organizations run shelters and offer help, support, training, and education so that women can be self-sufficient. They also fight to change cultural attitudes and push for legal reform.

The Tools of Justice

In Pakistan, for example, legal reforms in the past decade have slowly started to give women the tools of basic justice. The story of Nasreen and countless other women became a catalyst for two groundbreaking resolutions in the provincial parliament in Punjab in 2003. One prohibited acid attacks on women. The other abolished violent customary practices or vani, which include honor killings, forced marriages and women bartered into marriage to make up for crimes committed by their male family members. These reforms were unprecedented and moved forward in a parliament that is notoriously corrupt, traditionalist and patriarchal, with leaders who are not only collaborators but often directly involved in violence themselves.

The resolutions had a snowball effect. They created pressure on the federal government of Pakistan, then led by Pervez Musharraf, to amend the nation's criminal laws to protect women against domestic abuse. The following year, despite opposition from many religious leaders, a Women's Protection Act was passed that repealed the Hudood Ordinance, under which a woman subjected to rape, even gang rape, was accused of fornication.

Last year [2009], Pakistan enacted a Protection against Harassment of Women at the Workplace bill. None of this would have happened without the concerted effort of local women leaders, community-based organizations, NGOs [nongovernmental organizations], and the media, which together created enough public awareness and pressure to move the needle.

Now the needle may move again. The International Violence Against Women Act, a historic, bipartisan effort by the United States to address violence against women globally, was introduced this week [February 2010].

A Priority for the US Government

The bill addresses, for the first time, violence against women and girls through all relevant US foreign policy efforts, including its international assistance programs. It would support local efforts in up to 20 countries, assisting in public awareness and health campaigns; shelters; education, training, and economic empowerment programs for women, as well as legal re-

---

Domestic Violence against Women Worldwide

Japan
- 59% of 796 women surveyed in 1993 reported being physically abused by their partner.

India
- Up to 45% of married men acknowledged physically abusing their wives, according to a 1996 survey of 6,902 men in the state of Uttar Pradesh.

Egypt
- 35% of women (a nationally representative sample of women) reported being beaten by their husband at some point in their marriage.

Kenya
- 42% of 612 women surveyed in one district reported having been beaten by a partner; of those, 58% reported that they were beaten often or sometimes.

Mexico
- 30% of 650 women surveyed in Guadalajara reported at least one episode of physical violence by a partner; 13% reported physical violence within the previous year, according to a 1997 report.

Poland
- 60% of divorced women surveyed in 1993 by the Centre for the Examination of Public Opinion reported having been hit at least once by their ex-husbands; an additional 25% reported repeated violence.

TAKEN FROM: UNICEF, "Domestic Violence," *Innocenti Digest*, June 2000.

---

forms. It would also make the issue a diplomatic priority for the first time, asking the United States to respond within three months to horrific acts of violence against women and girls committed during conflict and war.

Support from the American public is strong. A 2009 poll found that 61 percent of voters across demographic and political lines thought global violence against women should be one of the top international priorities for the US government, and 82 percent supported the International Violence Against Women Act.

Despite the odds women face, we, as advocates to end this global scourge, are always awed by their strength. There are countless examples of women supporting each other to overcome the bleakest of circumstances. Helping them become economically empowered and providing protection and access to justice will enable these women to create societies that are more tolerant, less violent, less extremist, and more humane and socially just. Passing the International Violence Against Women Act could truly be a life-changing force for millions of women and girls like Nasreen around the world.

> "As high-tech tools become increasingly ingrained in our everyday lives, abusers and stalkers are increasingly using them to track and intimidate their victims."

The Use of Technology by Domestic Abusers Is Increasing

Information Week

In the following viewpoint, the editors of Information Week *claim that the number of abusers using technology to intimidate and monitor their victims is growing. For example, the authors maintain, some abusers use spyware to track Internet searches that may reveal research on abuse shelters or the purchase of tickets for travel, thus revealing plans to leave the abuser. In addition, they assert, some use cell phones to send threatening messages and use GPS devices to track their victims' movements. The authors recommend that victims install strong security software, use community computers to make escape plans, and save threatening messages as evidence.* Information Week *is a business technology news magazine.*

As you read, consider the following questions:

1. In the opinion of *Information Week* editors, why is it important to be aware of the tools that can be used against victims?

2. According to Cindy Southworth, as cited by the authors, what is the most dangerous time for victims of domestic abuse?

3. In Southworth's view, as cited by *Information Week*, what has been the biggest message her organization has been sending to law enforcement officers about the use of technology to control and abuse people?

A woman, looking to get out of an abusive relationship, goes online to buy plane tickets for herself and her two small children, and then she e-mails a friend about her plan to leave. As she works to secretly put things in order, she doesn't realize her husband has downloaded spyware onto the computer and will soon know everything she's planning to do.

Using Technology to Intimidate Victims

It's a scenario that security professionals and social workers say is happening more and more frequently. And this week [in mid-August 2007], a McAfee [computer security company] researcher is meeting with domestic abuse advocates to help them fight the growing use of technology in abuse and stalking cases.

As high-tech tools become increasingly ingrained in our everyday lives, abusers and stalkers are increasingly using them to track and intimidate their victims, said Cindy Southworth, director and founder of the Safety Net Project, an organization working to end domestic violence. Making women and men—as well as law enforcement—aware of the tools that could be used against victims is an important step in protecting them.

Tips for Survivors of Abuse

- If you use the monitored computer to try to research spyware or try to access anti-spyware scanners, spyware will log all of this activity and alert the perpetrator which could be dangerous.

- Try to use a safer computer when you look for domestic or sexual violence resources. It may be safer to use a computer at a public library, community center, or Internet café. . . .

- Trust your instincts and look for patterns. If your abuser knows too much about things you've only told people via email or instant messenger, there may be spyware on your computer. If you think you're being monitored by an abuser, you probably are.

National Network to End Domestic Violence,
Who's Spying on Your Computer: Spyware, Surveillance
and Safety for Survivors, *2007. www.nnedv.org.*

"We hear story after story from victims and police about abusers installing spyware to monitor someone's moves, like researching domestic abuse shelters or buying bus tickets," Southworth told InformationWeek. "It can be potentially dangerous and even lethal. The highest risk time for victims' injury or death is when they leave or just after leaving. [For the abuser], it's all about maintaining control of the victim. If he finds out she's planning to leave, that could be deadly."

Once a year, advocates and social workers meet to hone their skills. This week, they're holding the "Technology Safety Training of Trainers" conference, and Hiep Dang, director of anti-malware research for McAfee, is educating trainees on the latest spyware and other tracking technology.

"I want the social advocates to put themselves in the shoes of the attacker," Dang said in an interview. "It's important because they need to see how the technology is being used against the victims themselves. Knowledge is power. . . . It is pretty scary. This technology gives the attackers insight into their victims' lives."

Southworth said a week doesn't go by that they don't hear about spyware being used in a domestic abuse case. Abusers also are hacking into victims' e-mail accounts, while also using cell phones to send threatening text messages, GPS devices to track the victims' vehicles, and keyloggers.

She also said that using technology to control and abuse people is still new enough that many law enforcement officers don't take it seriously and fail to investigate. "Our biggest message [to law enforcement] is to believe victims," said Southworth. "Our experience is that all this high-tech stuff sounds like it's from a science fiction novel."

Technology Tips for the Abused

Dang offered tips for people who find themselves in a situation where they think someone might be capable of using technology to stalk or abuse them:

Everyone, regardless of their present situation, should have security software, including antivirus, anti-spyware, and firewalls, installed on their computers;

If a victim finds that an abuser has installed spyware on a computer, it should not be removed. That would let the abuser know that the victim is onto him/her, and it also should be retained to be used as evidence at trial;

If a victim is going to buy tickets or do research about domestic abuse shelters or divorce laws, do it from a public computer, such as those at a library or an Internet cafe;

Spyware has become more sophisticated, so it's often difficult to tell if it's installed on a computer. Victims should be suspicious if their abuser has knowledge of private online conversations or unexpectedly shows up at a location where the victim planned to be.

Periodical and Internet Sources Bibliography

The following articles have been selected to supplement the diverse views presented in this chapter.

Christopher F. Barber	"Domestic Violence Against Men," *Nursing Standard*, August 2008.
Denis Campbell	"More than 40% of Domestic Violence Victims Are Male, Report Reveals," *Observer* (London), September 5, 2010.
Centers for Disease Control and Prevention	"Understanding Teen Dating Violence," 2010. www.cdc.gov/violenceprevention.
Nancy S. Erickson	"Economic Abuse: A Form of Abuse That Needs More Scrutiny," *New York Family Law Monthly*, October 1, 2008.
Glamour	"It's Time to End Dating Violence," July 2010.
Jennifer Hahn	"Tracking the Abusers: Can GPS Protect Women from Harm?," Truthout, Summer 2008. www.truth-out.org.
Barbara Kay	"Domestic Violence Myths," *National Post*, June 2, 2010.
Mike Males	"Wildly Overhyped 'Tween Dating Abuse' Survey Recycled to Promote Fashion Designer's Products and Program," July 13, 2008. www.YouthFacts.org.
Greg Sagan	"Domestic Violence: Everyone Suffers," *Amarillo (TX) Globe News*, September 28, 2010.
Jessica Williams-Gibson	"Killing Black Women," *Indianapolis (IN) Recorder*, October 15, 2010.

CHAPTER 2

What Are the Causes of Domestic Violence?

Chapter Preface

Government funds dedicated to domestic violence until recently have been used primarily to help victims and to prosecute offenders. Some activists argue that more money should be spent on preventing domestic abuse before the damage is done. "Many programs today focus on helping adult victims, and prevention has a lesser emphasis, if it is addressed at all," claims Esta Soler, president of Futures Without Violence, formerly the Family Violence Prevention Fund. Things are beginning to change, however, as more is learned about the root causes of domestic violence. As researchers gather more information about the causal factors, the debate over the best use of funds dedicated to domestic violence has become more heated. Indeed, the controversy over which programs should receive funds dedicated to address domestic violence is informed by the debate over what factors contribute to the problem.

Those who agree that more funds should be devoted to prevention generally agree that children who grow up in violent homes are more likely to become victims or perpetrators. In fact, a twenty-year study published in the August 2003 *Journal of Consulting and Clinical Psychology* concluded just that. Studies also show that abuse in the home leads to other problems, such as drug and alcohol abuse, eating disorders, and other mental and physical health problems. If abuse in the home contributes to later domestic abuse, then prevention efforts may further reduce domestic violence, these analysts assert. Unfortunately, while prevention advocates generally agree about which prevention strategies will work, "we need documentation by researchers to back it up," claims Diane M. Stuart of the US Department of Justice's Office on Violence Against Women. The study of domestic violence prevention strategies is relatively new. Congress attempted to address the need for more data through its DELTA program: Domestic Violence Prevention Enhancement and Leadership Through Alliances. The responsibility for overseeing the program was given to the Centers for Disease Control and Prevention (CDC). According to the CDC, "Prevention requires understanding the circumstances and factors that influence violence." The CDC's goal is to study the success of the programs in its purview and explore the "complex interplay between individual, relationship, community, and societal factors, and . . . address risk and protective factors from multiple domains."

Fathers' rights groups and conservative organizations devoted to promoting family values believe that state and local criminal laws are adequate to protect victims. They argue that no further funds should be devoted to domestic violence. These analysts believe that many domestic-violence programs do more harm than good by demonizing men and destroying families. According to Michael McCormick of the fathers' rights group American Coalition for Fathers and Children, "We're spending nearly $1 billion a year to reinforce in the public's mind that men are indiscriminately attacking women." These commentators claim that funds would be better spent building stronger families.

As resources to support domestic violence prevention programs are increasingly strained at the federal, state, and local levels, the debate about the best uses of such funding will continue. Moreover, those who are responsible for distributing scarce funds will want to measure the effectiveness of prevention programs to determine what works and what does not. The authors in the following chapter debate what they believe to be the causes of domestic violence, views that in turn inform which programs work and the best ways to spend funds targeting domestic violence.

| "There is no one single factor to account for violence perpetrated against women."

Multiple Factors Contribute to Domestic Violence Against Women Worldwide

Sapna Kumari, Richa Priyamvada, S. Chaudhury, A. Singh, A. Verma, and J. Prakash

In the following viewpoint, researchers Sapna Kumari, Richa Priyamvada, S. Chaudhury, A. Singh, A. Verma, and J. Prakash assert that violence against women is a global problem with interrelated causes. Factors such as sex roles and marriage customs in some cultures contribute to acceptance of violence against women as a cultural norm, they maintain. Limited access to economic options in some communities contributes to domestic violence by keeping women from escaping their abusers, the authors argue. Violence against women also is greater in societies where women lack representation in positions of power, they claim. The authors of this viewpoint are researchers at the Ranchi Institute of Neuropsychiatry & Allied Sciences in India.

Sapna Kumari, Richa Priyamvada, S. Chaudhury, A. Singh, A. Verma, and J. Prakash, "Possible Psychosocial Strategies for Controlling Violence Against Women," *Industrial Psychiatry*, July–December 2009, p. 130. Copyright © 2009 by Medknow Publications and Media Pvt. Ltd. All rights reserved. Reproduced by permission.

As you read, consider the following questions:

1. In the opinion of the authors, why is a multilayered strategy needed to address violence against women?

2. According to the authors, what are some of the economic factors responsible for domestic violence?

3. What do the authors claim are some of the legal factors that influence violence against women?

Women, the fair sex, are considered to be the weaker sex and one of the most powerless and marginalized sections of our society. Violence against women and girls continues to be a global epidemic. It is present in every country, cutting across boundaries of culture, class, education, income, ethnicity and age. A growing body of research studies indicates that 20% to 50% (varying from country to country) of women have experienced domestic violence. A multilayered strategy that addresses the structural causes of violence against women is needed. Strategies and interventions attempting to address violence against women should be guided by 5 underlying principles: Prevention, protection, early intervention, rebuilding the lives of victims/survivors and accountability. When planning interventions, there are a variety of stakeholders who should be borne in mind. Key areas for intervention include encouraging women empowerment; advocacy and awareness raising; education for building a culture of nonviolence; encouraging active participation of women in political systems; resource development; direct service provision to victims, survivors and perpetrators; networking and community mobilization; direct intervention to help victims/survivors rebuild their lives; legal reform; monitoring interventions and measures; early identification of 'at risk' families, communities, groups and individuals; and data collection and analysis.

Violence against women is any act of gender-based violence that results in, or is likely to result in, physical, sexual or mental harm or suffering to women, including threats of such acts, arbitrary deprivation of liberty, whether occurring in public or private life. It is one of the most pervasive of human rights violations, denying women and girls equality, security, dignity, self-worth and their right to enjoy fundamental freedoms. Violence against women is present in every country, cutting across boundaries of culture, class, education, income, ethnicity and age. The global dimensions of this violence are alarming. Violence against women continues to be a global epidemic that kills, tortures and maims—physically, psychologically, sexually and economically. Everywhere, women are vulnerable to violence and exploitation. Violence against women is a manifestation of historically unequal power relations between men and women, which have led to domination over, and discrimination against, women by men and to the prevention of full advancement of women.

The Types of Violence

Physical violence includes hitting, slapping, punching, kicking, burning, cutting or otherwise harming the body.

Sexual violence includes rape, assault, forced prostitution, incest, female genital mutilation, sexual harassment, inappropriate/unwanted touching, etc.

Economic violence includes overwork, denial of ownership of property, withholding or taking away earnings, denial of inheritance, withholding education, unequal pay, not being allowed to work, etc.

Emotional violence includes verbal abuse, threats, insults, control, constant criticism, intimidation, humiliation, etc.

The Causes of Violence

There is no one single factor to account for violence perpetrated against women. Increasingly, research has focused on the interrelatedness of various factors that could improve our understanding of the problem within different cultural contexts.

The important cultural factors are gender-specific socialization, cultural definitions of appropriate sex roles, expectations of roles within relationships, belief in the inherent superiority of males, values that give men proprietary rights over women and girls, notions of the family as a private sphere and under male control, customs of marriage (bride price/dowry) and acceptability of violence as a means to resolve conflict.

The important economic factors responsible for domestic violence are women's economic dependence on men; limited access to cash and credit; discriminatory laws regarding inheritance, property rights, use of communal lands and maintenance after divorce or widowhood; limited access to employment in formal and informal sectors; and limited access to education and training for women.

The important legal factors are lesser legal status of women, either by written law and/or by practice; laws regarding divorce, child custody, maintenance and inheritance; legal definitions of rape and domestic abuse; low levels of legal literacy among women; and insensitive treatment of women and girls by police and judiciary.

The important political factors are under-representation of women in power, politics, the media and in the legal and medical professions; domestic violence not taken seriously; notions of family being a private sphere and beyond control of the state; risk of challenge to status quo/religious laws; limited organization of women as a political force; and limited participation of women in organized political systems. . . .

Although alcohol and poverty are often identified as causes, they are triggers or contributing factors to violence. They are not the root cause of violence.

Consequences of Violence Against Women

The physical consequences are physical injuries—fractures, concussions; poor health—chronic pain, gastrointestinal disorders, permanent disability; and death due to homicide or suicide.

The sexual consequences are unwanted pregnancies; sexually transmitted infections, including HIV; miscarriages; and low birth weight babies.

The emotional consequences are an unhappy relationship with partner; emotional distance from, and mistrust by, children; stress, depression, hopelessness, lack of satisfaction, panic disorders, low self-esteem; and drug and/or alcohol abuse.

The economic consequences are loss of economic productivity; fewer hours worked due to injury and illness; and reduction in family and community incomes as a result of costs of treatment.

The Impact on Children

- Children live in fear all the time

- Low self-esteem

- Problems in school, e.g., poor performance

- Violent behavior

- Abnormally sensitive

- Withdrawal from activities

- Sleeping problems . . .

Addressing Structural Causes

A multi-layered strategy that addresses the structural causes of violence against women while providing immediate psychosocial services to victims/survivors ensures sustainability and is the only strategy that has the potential to eliminate this scourge. When planning strategies and interventions, there are a variety of stakeholders who should be borne in mind.

At the level of the family, the stakeholders include women, men, adolescents and children. Within the local community, partnerships have to be developed with traditional elders, reli-

Some of the Factors That Perpetuate Domestic Violence

- Gender-specific socialization

- Cultural definitions of appropriate sex roles

- Expectations of roles within relationships

- Belief in the inherent superiority of males

- Women's economic dependence on men

- Limited access to cash and credit

- Lesser legal status of women

- Laws regarding divorce, child custody, maintenance and inheritance

- Legal definitions of rape and domestic abuse

- Under-representation of women in power positions

- Notions of family being private and beyond control of the state

- Risk of challenge to status quo/religious laws

Innocenti Digest,
"Domestic Violence Against Women and Girls,"
June 2000.

gious leaders, community-based groups, neighborhood associations, men's groups (e.g., village farmers' associations), local councils and village-level bodies. Within civil society, the range of partners includes professional groups, women's and men's groups, NGOs [nongovernmental organizations], the private sector, the media, academia and trade unions. At the state level, strategies must be designed in partnership with the criminal justice system (the police, judiciary and lawyers); the health care system; parliament and provincial legislative bodies; and the education sector. At the international level, the stakeholders include international organizations (such as the United Nations agency, the World Bank and the regional development banks). . . .

Violence against women and girls is globally one of the most prevalent yet relatively hidden and ignored issues. It is a health-related, legal, economic, educational, developmental and, above all, a human rights issue. There is a need for coordinated and integrated policy responses; implementation of existing legislation; and greater accountability from government; in order to eliminate this violence. In recent years, there has been a greater understanding of the problem of violence, its causes and consequences. Women also have to learn to be assertive and accept new roles for themselves. They have to develop an optimistic and hopeful approach to life. They need to be empowered through education, employment opportunities, legal literacy and right to inheritance. Human rights education and information regarding violence should be provided to them because this is a matter of their absolute rights.

"There is no 'type' of person who 'beats up' a woman (or a man)."

Domestic Violence Perpetrators Are Not Easily Defined

Diane Pietkiewicz

In the following viewpoint, Diane Pietkiewicz argues that there is no typical domestic abuser profile. People who abuse their partners come from all socioeconomic groups and cultures, she maintains. In fact, Pietkiewicz asserts, domestic violence is not so much about violence as about control of the victim. Early in the relationship, most abusers are not violent, and even when they do become violent, they rarely are violent in front of others, she claims. Because domestic abuse often is not obvious, public education is essential, Pietkiewicz reasons. Pietkiewicz is a public education coordinator for Domestic Violence Intervention of Lebanon County, Pennsylvania.

As you read, consider the following questions:

1. What disturbed Pietkiewicz as much as the tragic death she read about in her community?

Diane Pietkiewicz, "Abusers Don't Come in Neatly Defined Forms," *The Lebanon Daily News* (Lebanon, PA), September 6, 2009. LDNews.com. Copyright © 2009 by The Lebanon Daily News (Lebanon, PA). All rights reserved. Reproduced by permission.

2. In the author's view, how do abusers often appear to others?

3. What does the author claim is the community's job?

Recently, Larry Anthony Coletti was allegedly stabbed by Pamela Poorman. This [Pennsylvania] couple appears to have had a history of domestic violence that seems to have ultimately led to Coletti's unfortunate death.

Having read the account of the events that led to Colletti's stabbing and its devastating outcome, I was struck by one statement made by a neighbor that disturbs me as much as this tragic event. The article cites a comment from a neighbor that read "He didn't seem like that type of guy (to beat up a woman)."

As an advocate for victims of domestic and dating violence, I know one thing is true: there is no "type" of person who "beats up" a woman (or a man). People like to believe that they can recognize an abusive person simply by appearance. Nothing could be further from the truth.

The Myths About Domestic Violence

This is just one of the many myths about domestic violence that allows it to continue in our homes and in our neighborhoods. It cannot be happening to anyone around us, because we would "see" it—and when a tragedy occurs, we are shocked because there were no "signs."

We cannot stop domestic and family violence if we refuse to acknowledge that it occurs all around us. It happens at the same rate in all races, faiths and socio-economic classes, and between married and unmarried partners. It does not favor any particular group or class. It happens more frequently to women, but there are also male victims of abuse in some relationships.

It is not simply physical in nature; abuse can be psychological, emotional, financial, sexual and verbal. Victims are often isolated, cut off from family and friends because of their terrible secret. Abusers often appear as well-liked, confident, friendly, upstanding citizens because the facade is important in maintaining power and control in their life and in the abusive relationship.

The Abusive Relationship

That is the crux of this sinister dilemma: Abusive relationships are not about violence. Violence is only a symptom, a tool for exacting control and oppressing the victim. Abusive relationships do not begin with harsh words or physical assaults. They begin with a charismatic partner who says and does the right things, and the victim is usually swept off his or her feet by their "prince" or "princess charming."

It is only as the relationship progresses that the abusive partner's behavior starts to subtly change, and often these changes happen only in the presence of the victim. Over time, the abusive behaviors escalate and become more frequent and often result in physical acts of violence. What were first seemingly innocent comments and criticisms become magnified into verbal and emotional assaults, and in a manner akin to brainwashing, lead the victim to believe he or she deserves to be treated in this degrading manner.

The perpetrators of abuse know how to wield words and actions to maintain control over the victim; they use fear and manipulation to ensure silence, and often threaten to harm the family and friends of the victim as well. Victims believe that they cause or deserve the harm that is inflicted on them; they lose their sense of self and struggle to try to heal the relationship they believe they can salvage. They do not speak of the abuse because they are told no one will believe them.

The Danger of Looking for a Stereotype

Unfortunately, when people still believe there is a "type" of person who is controlling and abusive, the abuser may be

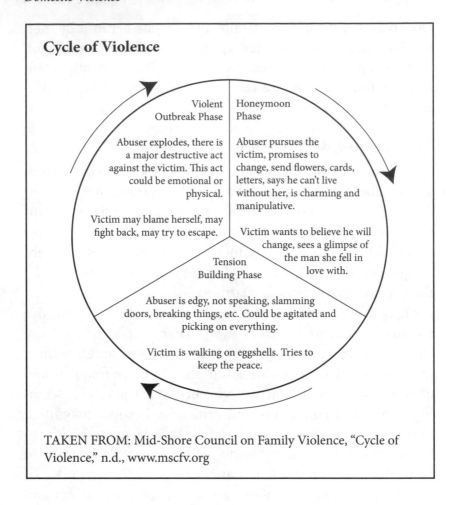

Cycle of Violence

Violent Outbreak Phase

Abuser explodes, there is a major destructive act against the victim. This act could be emotional or physical.

Victim may blame herself, may fight back, may try to escape.

Honeymoon Phase

Abuser pursues the victim, promises to change, send flowers, cards, letters, says he can't live without her, is charming and manipulative.

Victim wants to believe he will change, sees a glimpse of the man she fell in love with.

Tension Building Phase

Abuser is edgy, not speaking, slamming doors, breaking things, etc. Could be agitated and picking on everything.

Victim is walking on eggshells. Tries to keep the peace.

TAKEN FROM: Mid-Shore Council on Family Violence, "Cycle of Violence," n.d., www.mscfv.org

right—when there is no stereotypical abuser to be identified, why would anyone believe the victim?

[This] is not intended to brand Colletti as an abuser or to vindicate Poorman because she may be a victim; my intent is to remind the public that domestic violence is all around us, and it does not wear a label or identify itself. It is our job as a community to talk about domestic abuse and to teach our children that relationships are about trust and respect, not jealousy and control.

We need to make it known that when we hear fighting or see an argument we will not turn our heads and hope someone else takes action but call the police before it escalates into something that is irreversible. When an incident like this stabbing occurs, it is a terrible tragedy for every one involved and for the community. I offer my sympathies to both the Colletti and Poorman families—each in its own way is suffering a tremendous loss. I pray both families find strength and peace in the months ahead.

"We men have been socialized to continue a system of domination, dehumanization and oppression of women."

Male Socialization Normalizes Domestic Violence

Tony Porter

In the following viewpoint, Tony Porter claims that men have been socialized to dominate, dehumanize, and oppress women, thus normalizing domestic violence. Even nonabusive men perpetuate domestic violence by labeling the problem a women's issue, he argues. Porter asserts, however, that violence against women is a men's issue because male socialization—treating women as less than, as property, as objects—normalizes violence against women. Rather than separating themselves from abusers, well-meaning men should speak up and acknowledge that all men are part of the problem. Porter is cofounder of A Call to Men: The National Association of Men and Women Committed to Ending Violence Against Women.

As you read, consider the following questions:

1. What are the characteristics of the "well-meaning man," in Porter's view?

2. According to the author, what is deeply embedded in the socialization of all men?

3. What are some of the ways the author asserts well-meaning men give permission to abuse women?

You are a "good guy," not one of those men who would assault a woman. *You* would never commit a rape or hit your wife or girlfriend—you're not part of the problem. So how can you become part of the solution? You are exactly the kind of man who *can* help to end violence against women. So just what is a good guy? We call him a "well-meaning man." A well-meaning man is a man who believes women should be respected, including his wife, girlfriend and other women in his life. A well-meaning man does not assault a woman. A well-meaning man believes in equality for women, that women should be treated fairly and justly. A well-meaning man, for all practical purposes, is a nice guy, a good man.

My work, my vision, is not to "bash" well-meaning men. An assault on men is not going to end the assault on women. I seek to help men understand, through a process of re-education and accountability that, despite all our goodness, we men have been socialized to continue a system of domination, dehumanization and oppression of women.

Confronting Sexism

I do not come to this work as a man who thinks he knows it all or who "has it all together." I, too, am a "well-meaning man." For 20 years I worked in the field of alcohol/chemical dependency. Early on in that work I began to address the importance of cultural diversity in the field. After about three years I realized I had to go much deeper than a cultural diversity approach permitted. My work then began to focus more on issues related to group oppression, particularly racism. As I went about my business addressing the "ism" of race—racism and its relationship to alcoholism/chemical dependency, women I worked with began to confront me on my own "ism"—sexism.

At first I felt insulted, thinking (and sometimes verbalizing) "I'm a good guy, I'm no sexist." This remained my mindset for quite some time. Only through a series of events that challenged me did I begin to dismantle my cherished belief.

Over the next five years I immersed myself in learning, owning and addressing my sexism, as well as the collective sexism of men. I began to understand, to see that what emerged in my consciousness was that domestic violence, sexual assault and all other forms of violence against women are rooted in a sexist, male dominating society.

The Danger of Inaction

As well-meaning men, through our inaction, we allowed violence against women to be seen as a "women's issue." We spend little, if any, time addressing this epidemic. We look at violence against women through our own lens, a male socialized perspective that leaves little room for any true accountability for men. We don't mean to harm women; many of us have no idea what we're doing. Rather, we are just going with the flow, doing things as we always have. This approach has limited our ability or willingness to be concerned with how we affect women or how women experience us. One of the key things we have not done, and continue not to do, is listen to women.

Deeply embedded in the socialization of all men, well-meaning men included, is the conscious and unconscious ability (and sometimes desire) to tune women out, to silence them, to take away their voice, to not listen. Many men justify this action by saying that women talk too much, or they nag. We make no connection to the reality that if men would listen, women would not need to repeat themselves or be so detailed. As men, well-meaning men, if we choose to listen to

women and take their direction, we could actually end violence against women as we know it here in the United States.

Key Aspects of Male Socialization

Three key aspects of male socialization that create, normalize and maintain violence against women are: Men viewing women as "less than"; men treating women as "property"; and men seeing women as "objects." All three are major contributors to violence against women, perpetuated consciously or not by all men, including well-meaning men.

We must begin to examine the ways in which male socialization fosters violence against women. We must begin to examine the ways we separate ourselves from men who assault and abuse women, while simultaneously (through our inaction) giving them permission to do so. We make monsters out of them as a means of supporting our position that we're different from them. We remain focused on fixing *them*, pathologizing *their* violence, blaming family history, chemical dependency, mental illness, or an inability to manage their an-

95

ger, while for the most part, these are not the reasons men abuse women. It makes sense that we would expend the energy to "fix" them in order to maintain and even strengthen our status as "good guys." In doing so, we squeeze out the space needed to understand and acknowledge that violence against women is a manifestation of sexism. Once we can admit that violence against women springs from sexism, we have to acknowledge that all men are part of the problem.

Giving Permission to Abuse

The men we identify as "the bad guys," who assault and abuse women, largely do so by choice. Through our silence, these men receive a kind of permission to behave this way from those of us well-meaning men. We give men who abuse and assault permission in several ways: We stay quiet, "mind our own business"; we minimize the consequences and have limited means to hold these men accountable. We historically hold the view that violence is actually only physical abuse or sexual assault. Taking this position allows us to leave ourselves out of the equation and puts distance between the abuse and us. . . .

It is critically important to note that what I'm sharing is based on the teachings of women. If there is any contribution that I have to offer it is that I am finally starting to listen.

What I'm sharing also grew partly out of a series of discussions I have had with men over the last five years: men of all ages, ethnic groups, levels of education and family backgrounds. What did they all have in common? They were all "well-meaning men." I invite you to join in and examine your own role as a well-meaning man in this society. I invite you to begin to challenge other well-meaning men to join you. Together we can create the social change that will help to create a world that is more respectful of and safer for women. This work is long overdue. It's time to get started.

| "*Guns pose a uniquely deadly threat to victims of domestic violence.*"

The Availability of Guns Increases the Risk of Domestic Homicide

Nan Stoops and Sue Else

In the following viewpoint, Nan Stoops and Sue Else argue that guns pose a deadly threat to domestic violence victims. In fact, they maintain, 60 percent to 70 percent of those who killed their female partners used a gun. Recognizing the role guns play in domestic violence homicides, Congress passed the Domestic Violence Offender Gun Ban, which prohibits those convicted of misdemeanor domestic violence from owning or possessing guns, Stoops and Else claim. This reasonable restriction, they argue, saves lives. Stoops is executive director of the Washington State Coalition Against Domestic Violence; Else is president of the National Network to End Domestic Violence.

As you read, consider the following questions:

1. According to Stoops and Else, what do the stories of Rebecca Griego and Monique Vance show?

2. According to the authors, an abused woman living in a household with a gun is how many times more likely to be killed, compared with other women?

3. According to the US Department of Justice, by the end of 2006, how many people convicted of domestic violence crimes were blocked from gun purchases?

In April 2007, after months of stalking and threatening, Rebecca Griego's ex-boyfriend shot and killed her on the University of Washington campus. Just weeks later in Des Moines, [Iowa,] Monique Vance was chased down and shot to death by her husband as she ran to a neighbor for help.

While those crimes may appear to be isolated incidents, they are in fact intrinsically linked.

A Deadly Threat

Chances are the deaths of those two women won't be a prominent topic of discussion when the U.S. Supreme Court issues its decision in *District of Columbia v. Heller*,[1] the challenge to the District's handgun ban, in late June [2008]. But they should be, because as Griego's and Vance's stories show, guns pose a uniquely deadly threat to victims of domestic violence.

Domestic violence directly affects one in four women in every corner of this country. Each year, almost two million injuries and more than half a million emergency room visits are attributed to this kind of abuse.

1. The Supreme Court in *Heller* held that the Second Amendment protects an individual right to possess a firearm for traditionally lawful purposes such as self-defense within the home. The opinions did not discuss the domestic violence misdemeanor ban—the so-called Lautenberg Amendment, but the majority did add that "although we do not undertake an exhaustive historical analysis today of the full scope of the Second Amendment, nothing in our opinion should be taken to cast doubt on longstanding prohibitions on the possession of firearms by felons and the mentally ill, or laws forbidding the carrying of firearms in sensitive places such as schools and government buildings, or laws imposing conditions and qualifications on the commercial sale of arms."

Challenges to Lautenberg Rejected

The Lautenberg Amendment establishes a comprehensive federal scheme that is designed to prevent the use of firearms in domestic violence offenses by prohibiting the possession of firearms by persons convicted of a misdemeanor crime of domestic violence, as well as the knowing sale or disposition of any firearm or ammunition to a domestic violence misdemeanant....

While these provisions have been a significant source of legal controversy, reviewing courts have rejected all challenges to the validity of the Amendment, determining that its provisions comport with minimum constitutional requirements. Furthermore, while it is important to remember that there are tenable constitutional arguments that may be raised against the Lautenberg Amendment, the breadth of the decisions ... would appear to minimize the possibility of any future rulings invalidating its provisions.

T.J. Halsted, CRS Reports for Congress, *October 1, 2001.*

Domestic violence is also a crime. It accounts for more than one-third of all reported violent crimes in 18 states and the District of Columbia, and it claims the lives of three women each day.

And guns are undeniably the weapon of choice in domestic violence homicides. Studies show that from 1980 to 2000, 60 percent to 70 percent of abusers who killed their female partners used guns to do so.

In Washington state, where 359 people were killed by domestic violence abusers between Jan. 1, 1997 and June 30, 2006, abusers used guns in 200 of those murders. Women are more likely to be killed by guns than all other methods combined. Simply having a gun in the house makes an abused woman six times more likely than other women to be killed.

Keeping Guns Out of Abusers' Hands

For more than a decade, the federal government has recognized the devastating and deadly role guns play in domestic violence. In 1994, Congress passed the Domestic Violence Firearm Prevention Act, which prohibits gun possession by anyone who has a restraining or protective order issued against them in a case of reported domestic violence.

Congress strengthened its commitment to keeping guns out of the hands of abusers in 1996 by passing the Domestic Violence Offender Gun Ban. Commonly referred to as the Lautenberg Amendment, the ban prohibits anyone convicted of a misdemeanor crime of domestic violence from purchasing or possessing a gun. Statistics collected by the Department of Justice and analyzed by the Congressional Research Service estimate that by the end of 2006, the law had blocked more than 150,000 attempted gun purchases by people convicted of domestic violence crimes.

Seeing the promise of such restrictions in preventing domestic violence murders, state and local governments have followed in the footsteps of the federal government by enacting laws to prevent abusers from wielding guns.

These reasonable gun restrictions have been instrumental in protecting thousands of domestic violence victims.

Guns exacerbate an already pervasive problem, intensifying the violence and the likelihood that such violence will lead to death. Reasonable gun restrictions save lives by keeping guns out of the hands of individuals prone to harming others.

"Men were found to use more coercive control tactics when they were unemployed."

Economic Downturns Amplify Problems That Can Lead to Domestic Violence

Sheetal Ranjan and Chitra Raghavan

In the following viewpoint, Sheetal Ranjan and Chitra Raghavan claim that difficult economic times can create imbalances in families that may lead to domestic violence. In relationships in which men lose their jobs and women remain employed, traditional gender roles, in which men provide for the family economically, are challenged, Ranjan and Raghavan maintain. When combined with economic stress, they reason, this change in traditional gender roles can lead to violence. Indeed, the authors assert, studies show that employed women who have unemployed husbands are at greater risk of being abused. Ranjan is a sociology professor at William Paterson University of New Jersey; Raghavan is a psychology professor at John Jay College of Criminal Justice of the City University of New York.

Sheetal Ranjan and Chitra Raghavan, "The Economic Recession and Intimate Partner Violence," *Journal of Employee Assistance*, April 2010, pp. 17–18. Copyright © 2010 by Employee Assistance Professionals Association. All rights reserved. Reproduced by permission.

As you read, consider the following questions:

1. According to Ranjan and Raghavan, what does recent job loss data show?

2. What do the authors say that studies show to be the impact of income on intimate partner violence?

3. According to the authors, what types of services suffer in a tough economy?

The economic recession is affecting families in many ways. For example, recent job loss data indicate that men are losing jobs at a faster pace than women. According to the U.S. Bureau of Labor Statistics (BLS), 10.3 percent of males were unemployed in 2009, compared to 8.1 percent of females.

Challenging Gender Roles

In addition to stressors directly related to job loss, the disproportionate ratio of male to female unemployment has created an imbalance in families that may challenge traditional gender roles. Traditionally, men are expected to provide for the family economically, while women are supposed to play other roles. Taken together, these stressors and the unemployment imbalance can amplify an already tense relationship, potentially leading to partner violence.

The U.S. Centers for Disease Control (CDC) defines "intimate partner violence" (IPV) as physical, sexual or psychological harm by a current or former partner or spouse. IPV varies in frequency and severity and can range from one hit or slap to chronic, severe battering. . . .

Factors Related to Intimate Partner Violence

Many factors—being young, being female, belonging to an ethnic or racial minority or being an immigrant, having a low level of education, and being divorced or separated or living with a boyfriend or girlfriend—are associated with IPV. Social and psychological factors such as alcohol and substance abuse, exposure to parental violence, and jealousy are also associated with IPV. In addition, studies have observed a strong relationship between low income, high debts, job instability, perceived economic distress and IPV. A low income increases not only the likelihood of victimization but also the seriousness of the IPV.

In general, researchers agree that the discrepancy between earning level and need, rather than absolute income, is a better indicator of stress and subsequent violence. They also agree that partner violence is highest among couples where the male has no college education and the female is college educated and least likely among couples who are both college educated. In a study on employment, men were found to use more coercive control tactics when they were unemployed and their wives were employed. The same study found that being employed triples a woman's risk of being systematically abused when her husband is unemployed.

Alcohol use by either the perpetrator or the victim is a strongly supported risk factor in IPV literature. Research reports have indicated that IPV may be up to eight times more likely with alcohol use. Increased risk of IPV with substance abuse has also been commonly reported, with an odds ratio of 1.94.

Shifting the Balance

In a recession, when job instability, the risk of losing one's home, and indebtedness levels are all high, many individuals find it difficult to cope. If a man loses his job while his wife or girlfriend still has hers, complications can arise because employment is a "symbolic resource" in relationships and is directly related to the status of each partner in the relationship. In such situations, women may become the dominant decision makers, shifting the balance of the relationship during an already emotionally stressful period. A study by Macmillan and Gartner (1999) found that women's labor force participation lowers the risk of spousal abuse when their male partners are also employed but substantially increases it when their male partners are not employed. This finding has been found to be most relevant for traditional households.

Also, when a man is out of work, he is likely to spend more time at home, thereby increasing the risk of violence. Women, on the other hand, may feel trapped in abusive relationships because of financial uncertainties. In an abusive relationship, the abuser often financially enslaves the victim by "seizing paychecks" and/or taking control of the finances; in a recession, this is more likely given shrinking income levels and the fact that unemployed people can assert more control at home through their physical presence. In a tough economy, unfortunately, social services of all types are likely to be reduced because of lack of funding, further exacerbating the victims feeling of helplessness.

Consequences of Intimate Partner Violence

The CDC reports that victims of severe IPV lose nearly 8 million days of paid work—the equivalent of more than 32,000 full-time jobs—and almost 5.6 million days of household productivity each year. The Bureau of Justice Statistics reports that in 2005, 329 males and 1,181 females were murdered by an intimate partner.

While homicide is the most severe outcome of IPV, partner violence takes its toll on victims in a variety of other ways. Besides physical injuries such as bruises and scratches, the constant stress associated with IPV can have an impact on the immune system and endocrine functions of the victim. The CDC mentions the following as some of the disorders associated with IPV:

- Fibromyalgia;

- Irritable bowel syndrome;

- Gynecological disorders;

- Pregnancy difficulties like low birth weight babies and perinatal deaths;

- Sexually transmitted diseases, including HIV/AIDS;

- Central nervous system disorders;

- Gastrointestinal disorders; and

- Heart or circulatory conditions.

The psychological outcomes of IPV, like the physical outcomes, are primarily related to stress. Different studies report that psychopathological factors are both predicted by and predictive of IPV. The CDC mentions several psychological outcomes related to IPV, including the following:

- Depression;

- Antisocial behavior;

- Suicidal behavior in females;

- Anxiety;

- Low self-esteem;

- Inability to trust men;

- Fear of intimacy;

- Emotional detachment;

- Sleep disturbances; and

- Flashbacks to and mental replays of the assault.

In addition to physical and psychological outcomes, IPV affects the overall quality of the victim's life. Economically, women may find it harder to keep jobs or be successful at work. Additionally, they may become a victim of stalking at the workplace by their intimate partners. IPV victims may find that the victimization results in strained relationships with their health care providers and isolation from their social networks. Moreover, IPV victims are more likely to engage in behaviors that have negative health outcomes, such as risky sexual behaviors, substance abuse or unhealthy diet behaviors.

As the research makes evident, IPV has serious ramifications for employees and, thus, their employers.

| "Violence against women more often than not mirrors the culture of war and domination in our world."

A Culture of War Promotes Domestic Violence Worldwide

Amii Omara-Otunnu

In the following viewpoint, Amii Omara-Otunnu argues that violence against women is a manifestation of a worldwide culture of war in which societies resolve differences through violence. In societies that celebrate war and that make role models of war heroes, the fact that people turn to violence to control others and get what they want in their interpersonal relationships is unsurprising, she asserts. Indeed, many nations clearly value military might more highly than the education and welfare of their people, Omara-Otunnu reasons. To end violence against women, societies must build tolerant, compassionate societies that value peace and the rule of law, she concludes. History professor Omara-Otunnu is United Nations Educational, Scientific, and Cultural Organization (UNESCO) Chair in Human Rights at the University of Connecticut.

As you read, consider the following questions:

1. What did the *World Report on Violence and Health* find was a contributing factor to violence against women, as reported by Omara-Otunnu?

2. According to the author, what can be seen in countries where millions of people go without adequate food, health care, and education?

3. In Omara-Otunnu's view, what happens to children who are raised in an environment where violence is used as a common means of settling differences?

The facts are grotesque and chilling. Violence against women, who constitute more than a half of the human population, is a pervasive and cold reality of social life in most societies. Its human and economic costs are simply staggering. If we are to redeem humanity for a better world, it is imperative that we awake our consciences and adopt robust and effective strategies to eradicate this mutating pathology that has become an integral equation in the calculus of domination.

In Britain, around one in ten women experience rape or other violence each year. In the USA, about 17% of women have survived a completed or attempted rape. In South Africa, stories about violence against women have become such a staple of the media that they oftentimes simply numb moral sensibilities. A study by UN Development Fund for Women (UNIFEM) found that women in South Africa who had experienced violence at the hands of their partners were 48% more likely to be infected with HIV than those who had not.

A Worldwide Public Health Problem

In a groundbreaking and extensive research, the World Health Organization (WHO) concluded that gender-based violence, or violence against women (VAW), is a major public health and human rights problem throughout the world. The WHO *World Report on Violence and Health* notes that "one of the most common forms of VAW is that performed by a husband or male partner." The researchers found that cultural norms are a key contributing factor to the proliferation of violence against women.

And a recently released report by the UN Population Fund titled *State of World Population*, 2010, paints a grim picture of a global phenomenon of prejudice against women. It states that, "In all societies, to a greater or lesser degree, women and girls are subjected to physical, sexual and psychological abuse that cuts across lines of income, class and culture."

What seems puzzling is that violence against women has continued despite the formal adoption of many national laws and international declarations and legal instruments in support of equality of treatment and empowerment of women. How are we to understand the tragic paradox and address it?

A Culture of War

It is not sufficient to simply condemn and issue formal declarations for women's empowerment. The problem of effectively dealing with violence against women is essentially twofold.

In the first place, it requires that we properly diagnose the source of this festering pathology. At the root of the problem are values and means in society. Put plainly, violence against women more often than not mirrors the culture of war and domination in our world. It is a manifestation of the hegemonic [the processes by which the dominant culture maintains its dominance] values and the means people use in society to resolve differences or disputes. In a real sense, violence against women is a reflection of the poverty of ethical values, rational consideration and insecurity of men in society.

In daily discourse, it is found in the militaristic idioms used to express strength; in the metaphors employed to convey masculine virtue; in the way war heroes are placed on a pedestal, more or less as role models; and in glorification of war-related occasions, symbols and institutions. It can be detected in governmental priorities and resource allocation. And paradoxically, it finds sanction in some religious dogmas.

The degree to which a culture of war or militarism is more or less accepted in society can be gauged from, for example, national budgets. A critical examination of virtually all national expenditures shows a pattern of allocation of resources to the military and armament that dwarfs investments in productive sectors of society such as education, health care, agriculture, infrastructure, etc. In countries where millions of people go without adequate food, health care and education, the culture of war can be seen in the obscene purchase of armaments and their circulation in society. Even in those countries where the empowerment of women is taken seriously, it is interesting that resources given to the departments in charge of women empowerment is miniscule when compared to the resources devoted to organs handling the military or so-called security services, for example.

A Lethal Cocktail

When the modus operandi of militarism is adapted to interpersonal relations and grafted onto a habit of instant gratification, it forms a lethal cocktail. This is often manifested in a behaviour that insists on one's way without much consideration to other people's legitimate interests. Hence, when one is not granted what one would like, the tendency is to employ force to acquire what one would otherwise not be rightly entitled to, just as countries use military might to obtain what they would not gain through reasoned dialogue.

The simple and profound point is that violence against women is not in the DNA of men. Rather, it is a socially constructed component of power relations, which is bereft of ethical grounding or moral compass. It is a learned habit through socialisation. This might be illustrated by analogy.

Various studies have demonstrated that children who are raised in an environment where violence is used as a common means of settling differences over time internalise the mode of social interaction and regard it as normal. Once they regard violence as normal, they are likely themselves to be violent abusers in interpersonal relations. This is no less true of men in particular and people in general who are brought up in a culture of war.

It is therefore the triumph of the culture of war and politics of violence, which render the doctrine of rights and the ideals of human equality more or less meaningless for the great majority of people, especially for women.

Transforming Human Relations

And secondly, having identified the societal nature and source of violence against women, we should embark upon concerted and multifaceted education to raise consciousness, emancipate minds about the problem and transform the calculus of human relations. The task would require that in place of the culture of war, we should resolve to build institutions and a culture of peace based on ethical values of informed empathy, understanding, solidarity, tolerance, compassion, cooperation, reasoned discourse, dialogue and the rule of law.

Only an ecumenical [universal] movement informed by ethical values of moral and intellectual solidarity will alter the tide of history and violence against women and inaugurate a new dawn in which we treat one another in a spirit of ubuntu.[1]

1. Ubuntu, believed to come from Bantu, one of the languages of southern Africa, is an ethical philosophy that focuses on people's allegiances and relations with each other. A person with ubuntu is self-assured and not threatened by others, knowing that he or she is part of a greater whole and is therefore diminished when others are humiliated, diminished, tortured, or oppressed.

> "Veterans with [post-traumatic stress disorder] are two-to-three times more likely to commit intimate partner violence than veterans without the disorder."

Untreated Veterans Are More Likely to Commit Domestic Violence

Stacy Bannerman

In the following viewpoint, Stacy Bannerman argues that until the military acknowledges the problem, the epidemic of domestic violence by veterans will grow. Because the military promotes a virtual code of silence, the fear of reprisals keeps many military wives and veterans from reporting domestic abuse, she claims. Nevertheless, Bannerman asserts, veterans who have post-traumatic stress disorder are two-to-three times more likely to resort to domestic violence. Suggesting that the military address this growing problem is not anti-veteran, she contends; indeed,

*directly addressing the problem will help provide veterans the
care they need. Bannerman is author of* When the War Came
Home: The Inside Story of Reservists and the Families They
Leave Behind.

As you read, consider the following questions:

1. Why does Bannerman claim the epidemic of veteran
   domestic violence is significantly higher than reported?

2. According to the author, what are some of the ways
   military wives and girlfriends have been abused in the
   past five years when their partners returned from Iraq?

3. What mentality within military culture and civilian society appalls the author?

The alleged abuse of pop star Rihanna at the hands of
singer Chris Brown is a "huge, teachable moment," according to Oprah Winfrey, who did a show about the topic.
Meanwhile, the military community and veterans' organizations want to improve education and reduce stigma about the
effects of post-traumatic stress disorder [PTSD]. Then why are
they so silent about PTSD and the escalation of Veteran Domestic Violence?

"Domestic violence among veterans has reached historic
frequency," Helen Benedict writes in her new book *The Lonely
Soldier: The Private War of Women Serving in Iraq.* "And post-
traumatic stress disorder rates appear to be higher among Iraq
war veterans than among those who have served in Afghanistan or even, many believe, in Vietnam. One of the symptoms
of this disorder is uncontrollable violence."

In January of this year [2009], *The New York Times* reported that charges of domestic violence, rape and sexual assault have risen sharply at Fort Carson, Colorado.

But the fear of repercussions and the immense challenge
of going against the Camouflage Code of Silence, which de-

PTSD and Domestic Violence

Studies have found that, in addition to more general relationship problems, families of veterans with PTSD have more family violence, more physical and verbal aggression, and more instances of violence against a partner. . . .

[Researchers C.A.] Byrne and [D.S.] Riggs found that 42% of the 50 Vietnam veterans in their study had engaged in at least one act of violence against their partner during the preceding year, and 92% had committed at least one act of verbal aggression in the preceding year.

Jennifer L. Price and Susan P. Stevens,
Partners of Veterans with PTSD: Research Findings,
September 25, 2009. www.ptsd.va.gov.

fines the Armed Service's refusal to acknowledge the war on military wives and women veterans, ensure that most domestic abuse is not reported.

Furthermore, the Department of Defense does not track off-post police reports or claims filed in civilian courts.

An Epidemic Minimized

Given the unprecedented deployments of more than half a million citizen soldiers who do not live on base, but have nearly twice the rates of combat-related trauma as active-duty troops and are more likely to be married, it seems obvious that the epidemic of veteran domestic violence is significantly higher than reported.

Case in point: Days after selecting her wedding dress, the fiance of a Marine Corp. Reservist with severe, untreated, post-traumatic stress disorder came home to find her apartment on fire, having been torched by her betrothed, after a series of harassing, threatening, and violent encounters. She filed for, and was granted, a restraining order. But she doesn't count.

The connection between post-war trauma and veteran domestic violence has been extensively documented in earlier wars. Veterans with PTSD are two-to-three times more likely to commit intimate partner violence than veterans without the disorder, according to the Veterans Administration. What remains unspoken is that spouses and girlfriends of male veterans with post-traumatic stress disorder are two-to-three times more likely to be victims of domestic violence than women involved with male veterans who do not have the disorder.

The disregard for domestic collateral damage is evident in this comment from Mike Matthews, a retired Air Force officer studying troops in combat for Army Chief of Staff George Casey. Matthews said soldiers with PTSD "tend to abuse alcohol and their spouses more upon returning from the war zone." Whiskey or Army wife: six of one, half a dozen of the other.

The Hidden War Casualties

In the past five years, hundreds, if not thousands, of women have been beaten, assaulted, or terrorized when their husbands, fiances, or boyfriends got back from Iraq. Dozens of military wives have been strangled, shot, decapitated, dismembered, or otherwise murdered when their husbands brought the war on terror home. These women are as much casualties of war as are the thousands of troops who killed themselves after combat.

There have been multiple spousal murders at Fort Lewis [Washington], Fort Bragg [North Carolina] and military bases across the country. The victims are human footnotes, not worthy of a place in the national dialogue about veterans, post-war trauma and domestic abuse.

The men who enlisted knew that putting on a uniform meant being willing to die for their country. But as a military wife, I can assure you that not one of us took an oath at the altar saying that we were willing to die for our country at the hands of our husbands.

There is nothing loving, honorable, or patriotic about taking a beating for your nation. I am appalled at the mentality within military culture and civilian society that seems to believe that talking about one of the most horrendous home front costs of war is somehow unpatriotic and anti-veteran.

Being pro-veteran shouldn't require complicity with or tacit consent to the increasing incidents of domestic violence, rape, and sexual assault perpetrated by veterans. If domestic violence is never acceptable, then we can't make exceptions when military wives and girlfriends are the victims.

If we're serious about addressing domestic violence, PTSD, and taking care of this country's veterans, then we have to get honest about what's really going on in military families. Sometimes the truth hurts. But, to quote Oprah, "Love shouldn't."

"Judges say they have seen a startling rise in the number of domestic abuse . . . cases involving immigrant, refugee and Muslim families."

Some Immigrant Cultures Condone Behavior That Is Considered Domestic Violence in the United States

Sandra Tan

In the following viewpoint, Sandra Tan argues that some immigrants are facing prosecution in the United States because domestic violence is a common cultural practice in their native countries. In addition, fearing police intervention, many immigrant victims do not report or seek help for abuse, she asserts. While independence and individual freedom are strongly valued in the United States, some cultures emphasize obedience, Tan claims. Moreover, she explains, in some cultures, family problems are a private affair and to bring attention to them is shameful. Thus, public education and collaboration among legal and child and family advocates is necessary to help immigrant victims, she reports. Tan is a staff writer for the Buffalo News *in New York.*

As you read, consider the following questions:

1. In Tan's view, how do some foreign abusers hold their victims hostage?

2. What additional burden do social service and legal advocates say immigrants and refugees face, according to Tan?

3. According to the author, how can troubled families protect themselves without leaving a criminal conviction on an immigrant's record?

A refugee from Somalia was accused of trying to sell her 16-year-old daughter into marriage against her will.

Social Services took another Somali couple's six children because the father belt-whipped his 8-year-old son and tied him up for misbehaving in school.

A Yemeni husband beat his wife and threw her down the stairs for talking back to him in front of the family.

"How else can I teach her how to behave?" the bewildered man asked in court.

A Rise in Abuse Cases Among Immigrants

These and other cases like them are raising the concerns of judges, lawyers and human services providers in Buffalo [New York].

Erie County Family Court judges say they have seen a startling rise in the number of domestic abuse and juvenile delinquency cases involving immigrant, refugee and Muslim families who want help but fear police intervention.

In the immigrants' native countries, these incidents would be considered common social and cultural practices. But in their new home, they are classified as abuse and felony assault.

"We don't come from another city; we come from another planet," said Burma refugee Law Eh Soe. "In Burma, you can hit your wife or kid, but here, it's a crime."

Many foreign abusers hold victims hostage by threatening their immigration status in this country, said Shea Post, the victim services outreach coordinator for the International Institute resettlement agency. Language is also a major barrier.

"It's common for us to work with women who are terrified of being hurt or killed," Post said, "terrified of being ostracized by their community if they come forward, who have no idea about how our system works."

Soe added that services such as counseling are culturally unrecognizable to foreigners from conflict-ridden countries who liken extensive personal questioning to interrogation.

With more than 800 new refugees resettling in the Buffalo area each year, and nearly 1,500 expected next year [2011], the question of how to work with non-native residents struggling with family violence has become a growing challenge for those in the court system.

The problem is serious enough that a special community and courts collaborative was formed 10 months ago to improve services to this newer population. The group recently hosted a daylong workshop in Buffalo for Family Court judges, lawyers and social service workers.

"In America, we emphasize independence and individual freedoms," said Family Court Judge Lisa Bloch Rodwin in her opening remarks. "This is in direct conflict with certain cultures that emphasize obedience to parents and authority. How do we bridge the gap between behaviors which are accepted between spouses in other cultures, but which are not acceptable or legal here?"

In the 2 ½ years she's been judge, Rodwin said, she's seen at least a doubling of cases involving newcomers to the country and culturally isolated Muslims, noting that child neglect, abuse, family violence and juvenile delinquency are rampant.

These issues certainly are not confined to immigrants and refugees. Domestic violence and child neglect reach across all ethnicities and income levels.

Facing Additional Burdens

However, social service and legal advocates say immigrants and refugees face additional burdens of cultural differences, post-traumatic stress, generational power struggles, language barriers, immigrant community pressure and family isolation.

This country's dim view of corporal punishment, its acceptance of women's rights, and the criminalization of certain family behaviors are often lost on culturally insulated families who come from places where laws against family violence are nonexistent or unenforced.

Kenneth Gibbons, a lawyer who defends many immigrants accused of family violence crimes, said his clients often have a glorified view of this country and are completely shocked when they land in jail on family offense charges.

"They find themselves in court and charged with things that aren't culturally considered wrong in their countries," he said.

In addition, immigrant parents accustomed to complete obedience from their children find themselves in a losing power struggle as their children become Americanized and abandon their parents' cultural values in favor of the individualistic cultural norms of the United States.

"This is where the tensions happen," said Awadiya Yahyia, a refugee from the Darfur region of Sudan who spoke at the workshop.

Lining the Path to Violence

Those tensions can line the path to family violence and crime.

Lawyer Eli Ciambrone defended a Somali mother who was accused by her daughter of beating her and trying to sell her into an arranged marriage for $5,000.

The mother denied the charges, saying she was just trying to keep her daughter from dating another Somali refugee who came from a rival clan—an act that would have resulted in her daughter's execution in her home country.

The daughter later recanted and returned to live with her mother, but Ciambrone found herself fighting Social Services to keep the mother from pleading guilty to charges that could have eventually led to deportation by the Department of Homeland Security.

Another lawyer, Wallace Wiens of Neighborhood Legal Services, recounted an incident where an African refugee's disabled daughter wound up pregnant by another local male refugee, and questions of consent arose.

The grandmother, who was seeking custody, did not comprehend that lack of consent would be considered a crime in this country. She was pressured by male elders to let the matter drop and allow the father to have the child, Wiens said.

Given the tribal culture the woman came from, the lawyer said, deciding to place faith in the foreign court system was an act of courage. She was awarded custody.

"Domestic violence in just about any culture is a taboo issue, and if you're a minority here, you don't want to portray the culture that you're from in a negative light," said April Arman, who co-founded RAMAHA in 2006, a local Muslim support group for abuse victims.

Advocates said many victims come from cultures where airing family problems is considered shameful and family unity is paramount.

Getting the Word Out

But more local communities are learning that Family Court can provide orders of protection and other services through civil dispositions that can assist troubled families without leaving a criminal conviction on an immigrant's record.

"The word is getting out in domestic violence cases that you can get relief without pressing charges," Rodwin said.

The recent daylong workshop spearheaded by Rodwin and the Western New York Muslim and Immigrant Community/Family Court Collaborative, included sessions on immigration law, use of interpreters, addressing the Muslim faith and cultures, the role of refugee resettlement agencies and perspectives from defense lawyers and child and family advocates.

Many in attendance grilled immigration law experts about what types of offenses and court dispositions could lead an immigrant to be deported in domestic violence and child neglect cases.

They also were given practical tips from Khalid Qazi, president of the Muslim Public Affairs Council of Western New York, and Arman about how to interview Muslim families and work with less-Americanized victims in a culturally sensitive way.

They differentiated between cultural standards and the actual teachings of the Islamic faith, which condemns family violence.

"Domestic violence is not acceptable in Islam, or really any faith tradition," Arman said.

Paula Feroleto, administrative judge for the eight-county 8th Judicial District in Western New York, praised the recent workshop for its enlightening topic.

She said, "I think education promoted understanding."

Periodical and Internet Sources Bibliography

The following articles have been selected to supplement the diverse views presented in this chapter.

America	"Behind Closed Doors," March 8, 2010.
M.C. Black and M.J. Breiding	"Adverse Health Conditions and Health Risk Behaviors Associated with Intimate Partner Violence—United States, 2005," *Morbidity and Mortality Weekly Report*, February 8, 2008.
Stephanie Booth	"The Most Dangerous Time in a Relationship: A Certain Type of Man Becomes Violent If a Woman Breaks Up with Him," *Cosmopolitan*, August 2007.
Leah Bromfield	"Violence, Abuse and Neglect," *Family Matters*, Summer 2010.
Consumer Health News	"Teen Boys Who Attempt Suicide More Likely to Abuse as Adults; Men with This History Are More Prone to Hit and Injure Partner, Study Shows," June 14, 2010.
Mark De La Hey	"Gender Differences Seen in Consequences of Domestic Violence," *CrossCurrents: The Journal of Addiction and Mental Health*, Autumn 2006.
New York Times	"Gun Sense and Nonsense," February 28, 2009.
Karen Painter	"Domestic Violence—Why Does She Stay?," *Catholic Woman*, November/December 2010.
Tanya P. Roberts	"Alcohol Has Big Role in Domestic Violence," October 30, 2009. www.jdnews.com.
Nicole Sotelo	"Women Hit Hardest in Bad Economy," *National Catholic Reporter*, April 17, 2009.

OPPOSING
VIEWPOINTS®
SERIES

CHAPTER 3

What Policies Best Address Domestic Violence?

Chapter Preface

Only in recent decades have police officers and judges taken domestic violence seriously as a crime. Through most of the nation's history, people considered domestic violence a family problem best resolved privately. During the civil rights and women's rights movements of the 1960s and 1970s, attitudes began to change. People began to see domestic violence as a criminal act. The passage of the Violence Against Women Act (VAWA) in 1994 had a significant impact on attitudes within the criminal justice system. VAWA provides funding for training programs for police officers, judges, and prosecutors to help them better understand domestic violence.

Nevertheless, some in the criminal justice system refuse to recognize domestic violence as a crime and remain unwilling to help victims. For example, Maryland district court judge Richard Palumbo, who has since been removed from the bench, dismissed a request for a restraining order against Yvette Cade's estranged husband, who later entered the store where she worked, doused her with gasoline, and set her on fire. In still another case, this same judge asked a woman to speak up in his courtroom, although he had been told her husband had crushed her voice box. One of the controversies about which policies best address domestic violence is whether the criminal justice system is doing enough to protect victims of domestic violence. Some activists claim more needs to be done to educate judges and police officers. Others believe that such programs simply reinforce the view that only women are victims.

Since VAWA put a spotlight on domestic violence, more than three hundred judicial systems across the nation have created domestic violence courts. Many law schools now provide courses on domestic violence. Nevertheless, some states do not require that police officers, judges, or lawyers be trained. Moreover, as many as 80 percent of domestic violence victims do not have a lawyer to help them through the legal system. Adding to the problem is the commonly held perception that responding to domestic violence calls is dangerous. While no study yet proves that responding to such calls is dangerous, because some police officers believe these situations to be more dangerous, officers often wait for backup. Although John Terrill, spokesperson for the National Association of Police Organizations, denies that police officers treat domestic violence differently, activists believe that more training is necessary.

Opponents of judicial domestic violence education programs argue that these programs lead to unfair results for men. Some argue that women use these programs to gain the upper hand in child custody or divorce proceedings. According to attorney Lisa Scott, VAWA, the act that funds many of these programs, "has little to do with violence and much to do with divorce court." The American Coalition for Fathers and Children agrees. Women who go to domestic violence shelters are first advised to obtain a protective order, these commentators claim. In custody and divorce cases, they assert, a protective order, also known as a restraining order, makes it appear that the man is abusive even if there is no evidence to support the allegation. These analysts believe that current criminal statutes are adequate to protect domestic violence victims without laws and programs that support the view that women are victims and therefore more entitled to equal rights than fathers.

Clearly, the debate continues over which policies best address domestic violence, including questions about whether judicial education programs are effective tools. The authors in the following chapter debate these and other issues in answer to the question: What policies best address domestic violence?

"It is time to invest additional resources to ... help families and prevent children from being abused and neglected."

Better Funding of Child Protection Services Will Help Protect Children from Domestic Violence

National Child Abuse Coalition

In the following viewpoint, the National Child Abuse Coalition asserts that with federal support child protection services (CPS) can protect children from domestic abuse. The abuse of children in the home remains a serious public health problem in the United States, the coalition claims. Unfortunately, the coalition argues, funding does not match the need, and CPS case workers with enormous caseloads cannot make good decisions. Federal money would be better spent helping these workers to prevent abuse in the first place than spent to remove children from dangerous homes, the coalition concludes. The National Child Abuse Coalition coordinates federal advocacy efforts on behalf of abused and neglected children.

National Child Abuse Coalition, testimony submitted to the Subcommittee on Healthy Families and Communities, Committee on Education and Labor, US House of Representatives, regarding the reauthorization of the Child Abuse Prevention and Treatment Act (CAPTA), November 5, 2009. SocialWorkers.org. Copyright © 2009 by National Association of Social Workers. All rights reserved. Reproduced by permission.

As you read, consider the following questions:

1. In the opinion of the coalition, how many reports of suspected child abuse and neglect did CPS agencies receive in 2007?

2. According to the author, whom are federal child welfare laws heavily weighted to protect?

3. According to the viewpoint, what issues does the coalition propose should be addressed by Child Abuse Prevention and Treatment Act funds?

The National Child Abuse Coalition, representing a collaboration of national organizations committed to strengthening the federal response to the protection of children and the prevention of child abuse and neglect, calls on Congress to reauthorize the Child Abuse Prevention and Treatment Act (CAPTA) programs to provide the core federal policy and support for: strengthening the child protective services (CPS) infrastructure. . . .

A Serious Public Health Problem

Child maltreatment is a serious public health problem. The U.S. Department of Health and Human Services (HHS) reports that CPS agencies in 2007 received 3.2 million reports of suspected child abuse and neglect. Following the investigation of 1.97 million of these reports, an estimated 794,000 of these reports were found to be victims of abuse and neglect. Overall, the youngest children suffer the highest rate of victimization. Infants aged birth to 1 year are the most vulnerable victims of abuse and neglect, with a rate of victimization of 21.9 per 1,000 children. Slightly more than 42 percent of children who died of abuse or neglect had not reached their first birthday, and more than three-quarters of children who were killed (75.7 percent) were younger than 4 years of age. Fatalities due to child abuse and neglect claimed the lives of an estimated

1,760 children in 2007 (compared to 1,530 in 2006 and 1,460 children in 2005)—5 deaths each day. Indeed the actual number of child fatalities is believed to be much higher than these official statistics suggest.

These are the abused and neglected children who come to the attention of communities across the country for protection from further, even more serious harm. HHS also reports that many more children—whether known or unknown to protective services—are abused and neglected each year: According to the Third National Incidence Study of Child Abuse and Neglect, an estimated 2.8 million children are the victims of abuse and neglect in the United States. These numbers—and the lives of these children—cannot be taken lightly or dismissed.

In times of economic hardship such as these [in 2009], communities are challenged to protect vulnerable children from abuse and neglect and support parents in economic distress. Over the years, experience, shown through research, reveals that rates of child abuse are higher in areas with unusually high unemployment rates, and that increases in child abuse are preceded by periods of high job loss. The National Research Council has identified unemployment among the stresses associated with child maltreatment.

Keeping Children Safe

Preventing the abuse and neglect of children from happening in the first place will keep children safe and avert the consequences of child maltreatment. Research into the results later in life for children who have been maltreated show that:

1. Child abuse prevention can help to prevent crime. Victims of child abuse are more likely to become juvenile offenders, teenage runaways, and adult criminals later in life.

2. Ensuring that children are ready to learn means ensuring that children are safe at home. Abused and neglected children may experience poor prospects for success in school, typically suffering language and other developmental delays, and a disproportionate amount of incompetence and failure.

3. Preventing child abuse can help to prevent disabling conditions in children. Physical abuse of children can result in brain damage, mental retardation, cerebral palsy, and learning disorders.

4. Preventing child abuse helps prevent serious illnesses later in life. Research links childhood abuse with adult behaviors which result in the development of chronic diseases that cause death and disability.

We know that prevention works. Communities across the country have developed preventive services which show success in support programs for new parents, parent education, respite and crisis care, home visitor services, parent mutual support, and family support services.

Evaluations of home visiting services have shown positive effects in the areas of parenting and child abuse and neglect, birth outcomes, and health care. Crisis nurseries have been demonstrated to protect children against abuse at home. According to a recent evaluation funded by the HHS Children's Bureau analyzing the number of substantiated reports of child maltreatment in families using crisis nurseries with a comparison group of families for whom crisis respite services were unavailable, the families receiving crisis respite services were far less likely to ever have a substantiated report of maltreatment than the families without nursery services. According to a nationwide longitudinal study conducted by the National Council on Crime and Delinquency funded by the U.S. Department of Justice, parents who participated over time in Parents Anonymous parent mutual support-shared leadership groups showed improvement in child protective factors and reduced child maltreatment and other risk factors.

The Challenge of Responding Adequately

The incidence of child abuse and neglect exceeds the capacity of our system to respond adequately. HHS reports that the average time from start of investigation to provision of service is 40 days. More than a third (37.9%) of child victims receive no services. According to the HHS report, "the efforts of the CPS system have not been successful in preventing subsequent victimization." An analysis of the factors influencing the likelihood of recurrence includes the following results:

- Children who had been prior victims of maltreatment were 96 percent more likely to experience maltreatment again than those who were not prior victims.

- Child victims who were reported with a disability were 52 percent more likely to experience recurrence than children without a disability.

Federal officials have repeatedly cited states for certain deficiencies: significant numbers of children suffering abuse or neglect more than once in a six-month period; caseworkers who are not visiting children often enough to assess needs; and failure to provide promised medical and mental health services. We as a nation can do better. A CAPTA-funded 2001 study shows that job stress related to the number and composition of a child protective service worker's caseload affects decisions on substantiation of maltreatment reports. The same study reveals that a perceived lack of service resources in a community may be tied to an increased recurrence of reports.

In the 2003 reauthorization of CAPTA, the basic state grant section was amended to require that children under the age of 3 involved in a substantiated case of child abuse or ne-

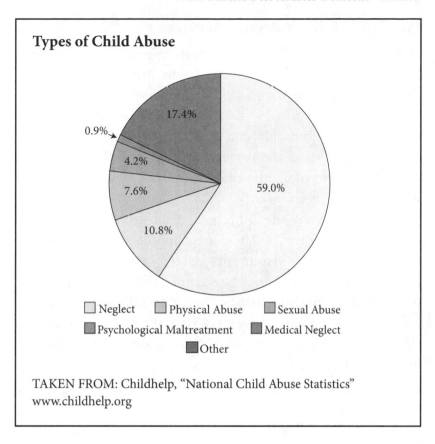

Types of Child Abuse

17.4%

0.9%

4.2%

7.6%

10.8%

59.0%

☐ Neglect ☐ Physical Abuse ☐ Sexual Abuse
■ Psychological Maltreatment ■ Medical Neglect
■ Other

TAKEN FROM: Childhelp, "National Child Abuse Statistics"
www.childhelp.org

glect must be referred to early intervention services funded under Part C of the Individuals with Disabilities Education Act. Unfortunately, the implementation of this essential provision has been sorely lacking. Part C does not have the capacity, without appropriate resources, to serve all children involved in substantiated cases referred by CPS. Nor do Part C agencies necessarily possess the knowledge and expertise to engage families referred by CPS. HHS needs to provide guidance to the states on implementing these procedures, and additional funding is essential in order to serve these children. Some agencies are making this work, but more needs to be done to attend to the important potential lying in these provisions in CAPTA.

Funding Child Protective Services

Current federal spending for child protective services and preventive services falls far short of the dollars invested in supporting the placement of children in foster care and adoptive families. For every dollar spent by the federal government in subsidies for the out-of-home placement of children, just 14 cents is spent on prevention and protective services. Federal laws have created a system of child welfare support heavily weighted toward protecting children who have been so seriously maltreated they are not safe at home and must be placed in foster care or adoptive homes. These are children whose safety is in danger; they demand our immediate attention. Increasing funding for CAPTA's basic state grants and community-based prevention grants will help to begin to address the current imbalance. It is time to invest additional resources to work in partnership with the states to help families and prevent children from being abused and neglected.

Unfortunately, far less attention in federal funding and policy is directed at preventing harm to these children from happening in the first place, or providing the appropriate services and treatment needed by families and children victimized by abuse or neglect. CAPTA must be reauthorized to respond to the current demand for treatment and prevention of child abuse and neglect. States continue to report record budget shortfalls and, for the first time in memory, state legislatures are cutting child welfare services and other supports to families to avoid spending deficits. As economic stresses increase pressures on families, we are concerned that over the coming months children will suffer as the funds for necessary services will go down. CAPTA, with a focus on support to improve the CPS infrastructure and our system of community-based prevention services, should be the source to help in providing those resources for prevention, intervention, and treatment.

Improving Child Protective Services

CAPTA should be the core source of funding for child protective services, yet it is not. CAPTA funding for basic state grants at the current level of $27 million is not up to addressing the scope of the need for support of CPS. The National Child Abuse Coalition believes that an annual authorized funding level of $500 million is a realistic approach to developing the CAPTA basic state grant program as a source of core funding for child protective services. A commitment at this level of funding will begin to help close the gap between what federal, state and local dollars currently allocate to protect children and treat child victims, and what those services cost.

CAPTA basic state grants are used for developing innovative approaches in CPS systems. This is potentially an important source of support for improving the child protective service system from state to state. Through the CAPTA basic state grant program, the federal government has the opportunity to step up to a leadership role in providing support for the CPS system infrastructure and to begin to rectify the imbalance in the federal government's response to the abuse and neglect of children.

States report having difficulty in recruiting and retaining child welfare workers, because of issues like low salaries, high caseloads, insufficient training and limited supervision, and the turnover of child welfare workers—estimated to be between 30 and 40 percent annually nationwide. The average caseload for child welfare workers has typically been nearly double the recommended level, and obviously much higher in many jurisdictions. Because our system is weighted toward protecting the most seriously injured children, we wait until it gets so bad that we have to step in. Far less attention in policy or funding is directed at preventing harm to children from ever happening in the first place or providing the appropriate services and treatment needed by families and children victimized by abuse or neglect.

Addressing Child Abuse Issues

In addition to authorizing meaningful appropriations for the basic state grants to help improve the CPS infrastructure, the National Child Abuse Coalition proposes to address through those grants a variety of activities essential to a responsive, efficient and appropriate protective service system, enabling states to improve their CPS systems through CAPTA grant support. In addition to the purposes for basic state grants in current law which address CPS improvements, the Coalition proposes that CAPTA funds be available to address the following issues:

CPS and family violence services collaboration: recognizing that domestic violence and child maltreatment coexist in 30 to 60 percent of the families among whom either is present, child welfare and domestic violence prevention programs should adopt assessment and intervention procedures aimed at enhancing the safety both of children and victims of domestic violence, including, where appropriate, developing and implementing collaborative procedures between child protective services and domestic violence services, in the investigation, intervention, and delivery of services and treatment provided to children and families.

Data sharing: to develop systems of technology that support the program and track reports of child abuse and neglect from intake through final disposition and allow interstate and intrastate information exchange.

Services to families: to promote the implementation of policies and procedures which encourage the development of differential, multiple responses for referral of family to a community organization or voluntary preventive services where the child is not at risk of imminent harm; and policies and procedures encouraging the involvement of families in decision-making pertaining to cases of abuse and neglect of children.

Linkages to animal welfare: to promote collaborations between the child protection system and animal welfare agencies in recognizing incidences of child abuse and neglect.

Legal representation: to require the appointment of an attorney to represent the legal interests of the child, as well as a guardian ad litem to represent the child's best interests.

Medical neglect: to extend protection to all children from medical neglect by removing language from CAPTA with the effect of allowing states to permit parents to withhold medical care from sick and injured children on religious grounds in the provision stating that there is no "Federal requirement that a parent or legal guardian provide a child any medical service or treatment against the religious beliefs of the parent or legal guardian . . . ," in accord with the U.S. Supreme Court holding that the First Amendment does not allow one's religious practices or beliefs to endanger one's children. . . .

Training

The connection between workforce quality and family outcomes was documented in a 2003 report by the U.S. General Accounting Office: "A stable and highly skilled child welfare workforce is necessary to effectively provide child welfare services that meet federal goals. [However,] large caseloads and worker turnover delay the timeliness of investigation and limit the frequency of worker visits with children, hampering agencies' attainment of some key federal safety and permanency outcomes."

It has been documented that a well prepared staff is more likely to remain in the field of child welfare, thus reducing worker turnover and increasing continuity of services with the family. Some social workers are able to take advantage of Federal assistance through the Title IV-E and Title IV-B programs of the Social Security Act. These funds are used to upgrade the skills and qualifications of child welfare workers through their participation in training programs specifically focused on child welfare practice. While these programs serve a useful purpose and must be preserved, we know that these two programs alone cannot support the entire field of child welfare workers.

A recent NASW study, Assuring the Sufficiency of a Frontline Workforce: A National Study of Licensed Social Workers, shines a bright light on issues related to workforce retention. The study warns of an impending shortage of social workers that threatens future services for all Americans, especially the most vulnerable among us, children and older adults. Key findings include:

- The supply of licensed social workers is insufficient to meet the needs of organizations serving children and families

- Workload expansion plus fewer resources impedes social worker retention

- Agencies struggle to fill social work vacancies

Congress should provide sufficient funds to allow for research, training, and evaluation of services in the child welfare system. Also, greater investments are needed to provide social workers with professional development preparation and ongoing training opportunities, particularly in the area of cultural competence. We believe that valuable employment incentives, including pay increases, benefits, student loan forgiveness, and promotional opportunities are essential for the development of a highly skilled human services workforce.

CAPTA has an important role in the federal response to the prevention of child maltreatment and the protection of abused and neglected children. Unfortunately, the federal role bears almost no relationship to the extent of the problem of child maltreatment in our society. While the numbers of children abused and neglected each year in the United States remain high, federal budgetary policy remains focused on pay-ing billions of dollars for the removal of children from homes where they are no longer safe. Relatively few federal resources are directed at helping states and communities in their response to protecting children at the first instance of harm, or preventing that harm from happening at all.

The prevention of child abuse requires intensive effort and the commitment of resources such as we rarely see in government, certainly more than is allocated to date through CAPTA. We are at a point now where we can act to improve upon the federal support and leadership. We urge the adoption of legislation to amend CAPTA in ways that will truly assist states and communities in their efforts to keep children from harm. We stand ready to assist this subcommittee and your colleagues in Congress in developing a responsive federal role for protecting children and preventing child abuse.

"The trouble with the child protective system in America is not that it hurts parents, though of course it does. The trouble with the system is that it hurts children."

Child Protection Services Hurt Children and Families

National Coalition for Child Protection Reform

In the following viewpoint, the National Coalition for Child Protection Reform (NCCPR) argues that the child protective services system hurts children by unnecessarily disrupting families. Removing children from homes based on false or trivial allegations disrupts the bond of trust that is necessary for healthy family relationships, the coalition claims. The system makes it too easy to remove children from homes and place them in foster care, which is no guarantee of safety, NCCPR reasons. When untrained and inexperienced caseworkers face a flood of false allegations, the author asserts, the children who need protection most do not receive the help they need. NCCPR is an organization based in Alexandria, Virginia, that advocates child protection reforms to promote family preservation.

As you read, consider the following questions:

1. In the opinion of NCCPR, what is the flawed image of child abuse in America painted by the nation's child welfare establishment?

2. According to the author, what have the child savers given untrained, inexperienced, sometimes incompetent caseworkers the power to do?

3. In the author's view, how does the rate of abuse in foster care compare with that of the general population?

Think of "child abuse" and what comes to mind? Probably a child brutally beaten, raped or tortured by a parent.

Think of "foster care" and what comes to mind? Probably a safe haven for a child of a hopeless addict whose mother just tried to sell him on the street for her next fix.

Think of your local agency responsible for dealing with child abuse, Child Protective Services, and what comes to mind? Probably an agency that supposedly intervenes in only the most serious cases, removes children from their homes only as a last resort, and makes one big mistake: Returning children to dangerous homes because some fuzzy-minded law requires it.

A False Image of Child Abuse

That is the image of child abuse in America painted by much of the nation's child welfare establishment.

That image is false.

By portraying horror stories of brutally abused children as the norm, America's "child savers" (a term they gave themselves in the 19th Century) have persuaded us to cede to them unprecedented power over the lives of children. We have given untrained, inexperienced, sometimes incompetent workers the power to enter our homes, interrogate and strip-search our children and even remove them to foster care entirely on the workers' own authority.

The child savers say they need this near-absolute power in order to protect children. They portray any challenge to their authority as a clash between the rights of children and the rights of parents. But the trouble with the child protective system in America is not that it hurts parents, though of course it does. The trouble with the system is that it hurts children.

It hurts children who have never been maltreated by disrupting their families, invading their privacy, and jeopardizing the bond of trust that is essential for healthy parent-child relationships. More than two million children are victimized by false allegations of child abuse every year.

It hurts children by making it too easy to pull them from their homes and place them in the nation's chaotic system of foster care. "Foster care is the garbage dump," says a woman who survived it. "That's what they do with kids when they don't know what else to do with them, throw 'em in foster care." The typical foster child was not taken from someone who is brutally abusive or hopelessly addicted. Far more common are children taken from their parents because the family's poverty has been confused with neglect. Often, these children bounce from home to home, emerging years later unable to love or trust anyone. Far from a last resort, foster care often is the first and only answer offered for every family problem.

And foster care is no guarantee of safety. Some children wind up sleeping in child welfare offices, others end up in institutions that would make [nineteenth-century social critic and author Charles] Dickens cringe. And the rate of abuse in foster care is higher than the rate of abuse in the general population.

Many of the children now in foster care don't have to be there. Some never needed to be taken in the first place. Others could live *safely* in their own homes if proper services were provided.

The Danger of False Reports

Perhaps worst of all, the system does terrible harm to the children who need help the most, those who have been severely abused. False and trivial reports flood the system, cascading down upon untrained, inexperienced workers who already have far more than they can handle, stealing their time and attention from children who really do need their intervention. And that is the real reason children "known to the system" sometimes die of abuse. Contrary to the claims of the child savers, there is no law requiring or pressuring for the return of a child to an unsafe home.

This is a system that destroys children in order to save them. But it doesn't have to be this way. The National Coalition for Child Protection Reform supports a series of measures to reform the child protective system from top to bottom. . . . These measures would reduce intrusion into innocent families, curb the needless placement of children in foster care, and free up workers to help children who really have been abused and neglected. Contrary to the claims of the child savers, these goals are not contradictory, they are complementary.

> *"Global Positioning System (GPS) moni-*
> *toring of domestic abusers . . . offers a*
> *way to enforce the terms of an order of*
> *protection."*

Restraining Orders Enhanced by GPS Monitoring Will Protect Domestic Abuse Victims

Diane L. Rosenfeld

In the following viewpoint, Diane L. Rosenfeld maintains that monitoring the movement of domestic abusers with global positioning system (GPS) technology can prevent further abuse. Traditionally, she claims, orders of protection did more to curtail the freedom of victims than abusers. Moreover, by limiting the areas of protection, Rosenfeld reasons, orders gave abusers the freedom to abuse women outside those areas. GPS monitoring can address this flaw and give law enforcement the tools to enforce or-

Diane L. Rosenfeld, "Correlative Rights and the Boundaries of Freedom: Protecting the Civil Rights of Endangered Women," *Harvard Civil Rights–Civil Liberties Law Review*, Vol. 43, 2008, pp. 257–63. www.law.harvard.edu. Copyright © 2008 by Harvard Civil Rights–Civil Liberties Law Review. All rights reserved. Reproduced by permission.

ders and appropriately shift responsibility for abuse to the abuser, she concludes. Former senior counsel at the US Violence Against Women Office, Rosenfeld is currently a Harvard Law School lecturer.

As you read, consider the following questions:

1. What does Rosenfeld claim is the underlying assumption of state protection order forms that require victims to identify sites of expected re-assault by a batterer?

2. According to the author, what is the common fate of many victims of domestic violence?

3. In the author's view, how does the Massachusetts GPS legislation work to protect domestic violence victims?

When Bonnie Woodring went to court to seek an order of protection from abuse by her husband—as so many women in this country do every day—she checked off boxes on the court form identifying six places where she wished to be shielded: her home, her workplace, her child's school, her child's day care, any place where she might be receiving 'temporary shelter,' and 'other.' For 'other,' she wrote in "stores (Walmart) within 50–100 feet." In effect, when battered women check off such boxes, they are selecting circumscribed areas where they may be free from violence, conceding the persistence of danger outside of them. The forms reflect the common understanding that such places are sites of expected re-assault by the batterer, but underlying this accurate assumption is a far more troubling proposition: the state is acknowledging its inability or unwillingness to protect women outside of these spaces.

Guaranteeing the Abuser's Freedom

As a society, we have come to expect that this is an appropriate response to a battered woman's pleas for help, but that expectation is deeply suspect. By granting an abused person rights to move freely only within these circumscribed zones, the state is implicitly granting the abuser the right to move freely in all the other zones. Although the state appears to be granting freedom and protection to a recipient of an order of protection, a more critical look reveals that it is not in fact offering much. Instead, the state is preserving a system of entitlements that guarantees a man's freedom of movement at the expense of a woman's. In effect, one might say that the restraining order has the perverse effect of restraining the liberty of the person protected by the order, rather than that of the person subject to the order. . . .

Orders of protection provide limited and unreliable protection from further abuse of the victim by the offender. Studies reveal that around a quarter of all orders of protection are violated and that those violations commonly go unpunished, leaving many battered women to fend for themselves. Aware of this under-enforcement, many battered women do not report violations of their orders, assuming (accurately) that the criminal justice system will not take their complaints seriously. Moreover, the alarming incidence of so-called "retribution assault," in which a batterer attacks his partner to punish her for seeking protection from him in the courts, highlights the hollowness of the order. Not only do the orders not benefit the victims, they sometimes expose the victims to even more harm. Batterers are well aware of this situation. Indeed, they often invoke law enforcement's lax response in specific threats to further harm the victim.

In Bonnie Woodring's case, John Woodring beat her again when she went home after receiving her order of protection from the court. There is no record of her reporting this violation. Bonnie went to the hospital, and when she left the hospital, fled with her thirteen-year-old son to a battered women's shelter instead of trying to go back home, even though her order of protection ostensibly gave her a legal right to be safe there. Over the next week, John called and e-mailed her repeatedly and sent flowers to her place of employment—all in violation of the order of protection prohibiting any contact with her. The night before Bonnie and John were to return to court for a full hearing on the order of protection, John tracked Bonnie down at a shelter and shot her to death in the kitchen. Her son was in another room at the time.

Predictable Homicides

Bonnie's murder at a battered women's shelter calls into question the safety of shelters and demonstrates how hiding from a stalking predator is often not a viable option. Her fate is all too common. With distressing frequency, domestic violence ends, not in escape and reconstruction of the woman's life, but in murder or murder/suicide. In the United States, three women are killed each day by their intimate partners. Approximately one-quarter of them are known to have had an order of protection. This murder rate is atrocious and signifies a grave deprivation of civil rights.

While the number of women murdered by their intimate partners is only a small percentage of women who report being beaten and abused, these murders have enormous symbolic value. They are the background against which so much sub-lethal violence is committed. Many battered women do not know whether the next beating will be a fatal one. Batterers know that their victims are aware that murder is possible and consequently terrorize them more easily.

Unlike most other homicides, domestic violence homicides are so predictable as to be preventable. The cases that result in murder are not a random sample of domestic violence cases. Death is far more likely when certain factors are present than when they are absent. When the state intervenes effectively in a domestic situation, it can prevent the violence from escalating. On the other hand, weak state intervention will leave bat-

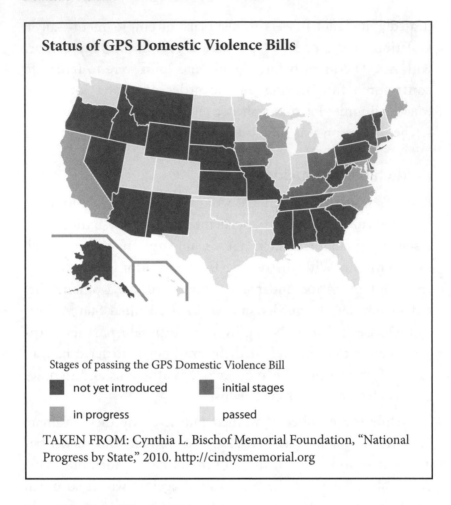

Status of GPS Domestic Violence Bills

Stages of passing the GPS Domestic Violence Bill

■ not yet introduced   ■ initial stages

■ in progress   ▢ passed

TAKEN FROM: Cynthia L. Bischof Memorial Foundation, "National Progress by State," 2010. http://cindysmemorial.org

tered women in a more dangerous situation—even worse off than if she had not sought help from the criminal justice system in the first place.

Looking for New Approaches

In recent years, the legal rights of women to be protected against male sexual violence have become weaker, not stronger. The Supreme Court has struck down the right to be free from gender-motivated violence and the right to compel enforcement of an order of protection from domestic violence. The probability that these decisions will be reversed in the near future is low. If we wish to right the current imbalance, we need to look for new approaches.

One promising initiative is the use of Global Positioning System (GPS) monitoring of domestic abusers. This technology offers a way to enforce the terms of an order of protection, holding both the offender and the state accountable for making the order offer the protection it claims to provide. This technology monitors the offender with an ankle bracelet to make sure that he does not violate the terms of the order of protection by entering forbidden zones where he would have the opportunity to re-assault or further terrorize the victim. Thus, rather than another legal-reform effort, the GPS initiative is a way to ensure that rights already promised by the justice system are delivered.

Several jurisdictions are now beginning to use GPS technology for domestic violence offenders. In Massachusetts, recent legislation explicitly authorizes the use of this technology in domestic violence cases. The Massachusetts legislation ("An Act Relative to Enhanced Protection for Victims of Domestic Violence") provides judges with the option of ordering offenders who have violated an order of protection to wear a GPS monitoring device. The bill allows the court to establish, as a condition of probation, geographic exclusion zones, which can include the victim's residence, place of work, her children's schools, or other places that she frequents. These GPS devices track the offender's movements to ensure that he is obeying the terms of the order of protection. If an offender enters geographic exclusion zones set by the court while wearing a GPS device, both the authorities and the victim are automatically notified. If the court finds that the offender violated the order of protection, it can order imprisonment, a fine, or both. The bill also allows the court to require the violator to pay the costs associated with the monitoring, which are estimated to be about ten dollars per day. The Probation Department is responsible for administration of the program. . . .

The Potential Impact of GPS Monitoring

Part of the potential for GPS to change the paradigm of domestic abuse is that it 'operationalizes' a battered woman's right to be free from the violent control of the perpetrator. It puts the law on her side by helping to enforce the terms of the order of protection and gives law enforcement knowledge of violations where previously they may have had none. Thus, it facilitates law enforcement response by pinpointing the location of the offender and by proving violations so that a court can impose more stringent controls on the offender.

Traditionally, law enforcement and the criminal justice system as a whole tended to discount the level of danger that an abuser presents to a victim. The use of GPS monitoring could make this danger clear by showing which perpetrators were violating orders of protection. This feature is important because violations of an order of protection signify that the offender believes he can violate the court order with impunity. The violations themselves are indications of increased dangerousness.

Whether a judge is willing to employ this new remedy may well reveal how seriously the judge takes the issuance of an order of protection. Moreover, the court may take the process of evaluating the domestic violence situation in terms of potential lethality much more seriously if there are real consequences for violating the order.

This monitoring . . . has the potential to disrupt the cycle of domestic violence and give meaning to an order of protection. Specifically, aligning responsibility with the person who committed an illegal act—rather than placing the responsibility on the person who suffered the violence—will enable a battered woman to stay safely at home rather than being forced to hide in a battered women's shelter, thus reversing the injustices in the current system.

"While judges certainly know that falsely obtained orders are pervasive, they care little for the well-being of the children who are harmed by losing their father for long periods."

Frivolous Domestic Violence Restraining Orders Hurt Children

Gregory A. Hession

In the following viewpoint, Gregory A. Hession argues that because there is no penalty for false claims of domestic abuse, courts often issue restraining orders without cause. While men suffer by being evicted from their homes following hearings that require no due process protection, the real victims are children unfairly separated from fathers, he claims. Obtaining a restraining order requires no evidence of abuse and is as easy as filling out a form, Hession maintains. When courts do require evidence, definitions of abuse are so subjective that accusers need not show real harm, he concludes. Hession is a constitutional and family law attorney in Springfield, Massachusetts.

Gregory A. Hession, "Restraining Orders Out of Control," *New American*, Vol. 24, No. 16, August 4, 2008, p. 12. www.jbs.org. Copyright © 2008 by the John Birch Society. All rights reserved. Reproduced by permission.

As you read, consider the following questions:

1. How easy does Respecting Accuracy in Domestic Abuse Reporting say it is to obtain a domestic abuse restraining order, as cited by the author?

2. According to Hession, why are falsely issued restraining orders of great concern?

3. In the author's view, what happens when lawmakers respond to political pressure?

One day in December of 2005, Colleen Nestler came to Santa Fe County District Court in New Mexico with a bizarre seven-page typed statement and requested a domestic-abuse restraining order against late-night TV host David Letterman. She stated, under oath, that Letterman seriously abused her by causing her bankruptcy, mental cruelty, and sleep deprivation since 1994. Nestler also alleged that he sent her secret signals "in code words" through his television program for many years and that he "responded to my thoughts of love" by expressing that he wanted to marry her.

Judge Daniel Sanchez issued a restraining order against Letterman based on those allegations. By doing so, it put Letterman on a national list of domestic abusers, gave him a criminal record, took away several of his constitutionally protected rights, and subjected him to criminal prosecution if he contacted Nestler directly or indirectly, or possessed a firearm.

Letterman had never met Colleen Nestler, and this all happened without his knowledge. Nonetheless, she requested that the order include an injunction requiring him not to "think of me, and release me from his mental harassment and hammering." Asked to explain why he had issued a restraining order on the basis of such an unusual complaint, Judge Sanchez answered that Nestler had filled out the restraining-order request form correctly. After much national ridicule, the judge finally dismissed the order against Letterman. Those who don't have a TV program and deep pockets are rarely so fortunate.

Is This American Justice?

Letterman's experience is replicated in state courts around the country thousands of times daily. Consider what happened to Todd, whose estranged wife went to court secretly and obtained a restraining order against him. She swore that three men dressed in purple Fathers for Justice camouflage uniforms broke into her apartment, pushed her violently onto her couch, choked her severely, and threatened her, telling her that she better not go back to court. She complained that these were agents of the husband, as he belonged to that group. She did not call the police, but decided to go to work. Later she collapsed near the entrance of a hospital emergency room in a dramatic flourish.

As Todd's lawyer, I provided evidence that her story was as phony as the one about David Letterman. The wife lived in a large apartment building on a main road with a busy lobby and a nosy superintendent across the hall from her. However, no one saw or heard the three strangely dressed intruders enter or leave during rush hour. The hospital records showed no bruises or evidence of physical assault. The court vacated the order against Todd.

Courts are easily manipulated by those pretending to seek protection from abuse because the political climate reinforces that men are abusers, and there is no penalty for false claims. Thus, they embolden applicants to use them for ulterior motives, such as to gain an advantage in divorce, to get custody of children easily without a family court hearing, or as a quick eviction process. Sometimes the motive is revenge or worse. For example, an order was issued against Brendan, father of two daughters, because he brought flowers to his child's home for her 10th birthday right after he sought enforcement of a custody order that the mother was routinely violating. Brendan was literally accused of "sneaking" into the yard to deliver flowers, nothing more, yet a restraining order was filed against him. This order was later vacated by a court.

An applicant can get a domestic-abuse restraining order for just about any reason. A report from an organization called Respecting Accuracy in Domestic Abuse Reporting (RADAR) suggests that it is as easy to obtain a restraining order as a hunting or fishing license. You fill out the forms and tell the judge you are afraid, and you get an order almost automatically. RADAR states: "The law defines almost any interpersonal maladjustment as 'domestic violence'; the courts then establish procedures to expedite the issuance of these orders."

A Lack of Evidence

The restraining-order laws of the several states are remarkably similar in their wording, as though an invisible hand were guiding them. They allow a woman to come to court secretly and claim that she feels fearful of "abuse" from a family member or person she lives with. The accused person is not there, and there is no requirement to notify him. There are no traditional rules of evidence, no opportunity for cross examination, no burden of proof beyond a reasonable doubt, no jury, nor even a necessity to have a story that makes sense.

The definition of "abuse" set forth in these state laws is always subjective, rather than requiring an injury or genuine threat. They all include a clause that expands abuse to include "fear of harm," often including even "emotional harm." Courts routinely issue orders on sworn statements like, "I just don't know what he may do," or, "he has a long history of verbal and emotional abuse."

A week after the initial secret hearing, a "return" hearing is held, where the defendant gets to tell his side of the story. He is usually allowed to present evidence and testimony, but it is often difficult to assemble needed documents and witnesses in that short period. Most of the temporary orders are extended for a year, regardless of the evidence, alibi, or witnesses offered.

To some judges, evidence is irrelevant; they just issue orders. Professor Stephen Baskerville, in his book *Taken Into Custody*, quotes Judge Richard Russell of Ocean City, New Jersey, at a restraining-order training seminar:

> Throw him out on the street, give him the clothes on his back and tell him, "See ya around." ... The woman needs this protection because the statute granted her that protection.... They have declared domestic violence to be an evil in our society. So we don't have to worry about the rights. Grant every order. That is the safest thing to do.

My client Mr. L's experience is a perfect example of this. I filed a motion to vacate the restraining order his ex-wife had against him, and she filed one to extend it, so the judge held a hearing to consider both motions—sort of. Here is the pertinent part of the actual transcript of the hearing to vacate the order:

Mr. Hession: Can you please state your name and your address for the record? [The Court argues with counsel as to whether Mr. L can testify.]

The Court: I don't believe I need to hear any evidence from your client. I'm going to deny your request to vacate the restraining order.

The hearing on whether to extend the order was no better:

The Court: Mrs. L—do you remain fearful of your husband?

Mrs. L: Yes. [Weeping]

The Court: Thank you.

The judge then extended the restraining order for a year, without Mr. L uttering his name on the witness stand, and with one generalized question to the wife about "fear." Judges who conduct hearings like this violate their oath to apply the law impartially and encourage the filing of false complaints—which is an enormous problem.

According to professor of accountancy Benjamin P. Foster, Ph.D, CPA, CMA, of the 4,796 emergency protective-order petitions issued in West Virginia in 2006, an estimated 80.6 percent "are false or unnecessary." Foster acknowledges the duplicitous nature of many of the complaints: "In divorce and child custody cases, a party generally obtains favorable treatment when the other party has engaged in domestic violence." In West Virginia, one incident of domestic violence, "which includes 'reasonable apprehension of physical harm' and 'creating fear of physical harm by harassment, psychological abuse,' . . . could impact the Parenting plan approved by the Family Court." On the other hand, a "parent must have *repeatedly* made fraudulent reports of domestic violence or child abuse" to lose favor with a court. (Emphasis added.) Just the "identifiable costs"—the cost for the state, not the victims—for these false reports was in excess of $18,200,000 in 2006.

A Drastic Punishment

Falsely issued restraining orders are of great concern because the punishment that is meted out to defendants is so drastic. After an initial secret restraining order is issued, the clerk faxes it to the local police, who then serve it on the defendant. Since most orders contain a "no contact" provision, the first thing the police do is remove the man from his home, with little more than the shirt on his back, just as Judge Richard Russell urged in his judicial training. Utterly taken by surprise, the man usually has no idea that the hearing took place, that the order was granted, or what he may have done to deserve it. The police are rarely sympathetic.

Most restraining orders require that the defendant may not contact the plaintiff directly or indirectly or get within some distance, usually 100 yards, of the alleged "victim." Of-

ten, wives place the children as "co-victims" on these orders, so the defendant cannot contact his children either. "No contact" means no phone calls, cards, letters, or even incidentally running into the person.

No reconciliation is possible once an order is issued because any contact is a crime and subjects the violator to immediate arrest and jail. Even indirect contact is a crime, such as asking a relative to help work things out. Many men have sent flowers to a spouse or a birthday card to a child, only to end up in prison. Once an order is in place, the state becomes the father in the family, pushing out the real one.

Most district attorneys, prompted by feminist political pressure, have a "no-drop" policy on prosecuting all violations of restraining orders, no matter how minor. Joseph found that out the hard way. His wife obtained a restraining order after telling the judge he had kicked a plastic cooler and slammed the door while leaving his house. She omitted the part about telling him she had found another man.

No abuse or threat had occurred, but an order was issued against Joseph anyway. While it was in place, the wife made 14 false criminal complaints about violations of the order, which resulted in some arrests. I had to go to court with Joseph again and again, and we somehow managed to beat every case. Only a dysfunctional system allows a complainant to continue to make such false allegations without any accountability whatsoever. . . .

The Impact on Children

Restraining orders especially impact the children. These orders are frequently used as a quick and dirty custody hearing, without the trouble of going to family court. In one minute, the father can lose the right to see his children for a year or longer. Children often get used as pawns in these situations, without any rebuke from a judge. While judges certainly know that falsely obtained orders are pervasive, they care little for the well-being of the children who are harmed by losing their father for long periods. The children often have no understanding of why they are being kept from their father because the father cannot even speak to them.

If dad works from home, as more people are now doing, additional problems arise. Under any order, he will be summarily evicted, and thus lose access to phones, business records, and equipment, without recourse. As a RADAR report puts it: "The man, now homeless and distraught, has only a few days to find a lawyer and prepare a defense." When a home business is involved, he now cannot earn income, although he may be ordered to pay child support, needs alternate living quarters, and may have had his bank account emptied by his wife. . . .

An Answer to Domestic Violence?

Domestic-abuse restraining orders came about because a certain number of abusers really do assault and batter their partners. Scores of studies have attempted to understand the problem and find practical solutions, but domestic-abuse restraining orders are a flawed solution that has made the problem worse.

First, they have identified the wrong culprit. Women commit abuse more than men do. The U.S. Centers for Disease Control and Prevention reports, "In non-reciprocally violent relationships, women were the perpetrators in more than 70 percent of the cases. Reciprocity was associated with more frequent violence among women, but not men." Psychologist John Archer reviewed hundreds of studies and concluded, "Women were slightly more likely than men to use one or more acts of physical aggression and to use such acts more frequently." While men are more often the victims of abuse, women are injured more often and more severely than men. Moreover, about two-thirds of the reported cases are minor, such as throwing a pillow. . . .

Whenever lawmakers respond to political pressure, a bad law is the usual result. Law has the properly limited purpose of insuring restitution to victims of those who intrude on the person or property of others. It has never been preventative, as domestic-abuse restraining-order laws seek to be, nor should it be. If true abuse does occur—a relative or nonrelative threatens to batter or kill you or actually does physically attack—you are already able to make a criminal complaint for assault (which is defined as a threat to batter) and battery. And a criminal restraining order will likely be set in place. These new restraining-order laws seek to prevent crime by identifying persons who may commit one, and stop it before it happens. However, this is entirely speculative, and cannot identify perpetrators with any reliability.

In our imperfect world, we settle for an imperfect system that uses fear of punishment, rather than preemption, as its primary deterrent, but look at the alternative. With unjust restraining-order laws, we are creating a legal system that victimizes large groups of innocent people. We need to develop a better system, before we completely lose control of the present one. Thomas Reed, Speaker of the House of Representatives in the late 19th century, said, "One of the greatest delusions in the world is the hope that the evils in this world are to be cured by legislation." Domestic-abuse restraining-order laws are a vain and delusional attempt to do so, and we need to eliminate them.

Periodical Bibliography

The following articles have been selected to supplement the diverse views presented in this chapter.

Caroline Bettinger-López

"*Jessica Gonzales v. United States*: An Emerging Model for Domestic Violence and Human Rights Advocacy in the United States," *Harvard Human Rights Journal*, Symposium 2008.

Vincent Carroll

"On Point: Usurping Justice," *Rocky Mountain News*, March 2, 2007.

Carrie Clingan

"*Town of Castle Rock, Colorado v. Gonzales*: The Value of a Restraining Order," *Journal of Gender, Race, and Justice*, Winter 2007.

Corrie Cutrer

"When Someone You Love Is Abused: What You Need to Know and How You Can Make a Difference," *Today's Christian Woman*, May/June 2009.

Amilia Duchon-Voyles and Liz Welch

"Lives: Safe Call; Taking the First Step Away from a Dangerous Home," *New York Times Magazine*, October 24, 2010.

Kim Gandy

"No Woman, No Culture Immune to Violence Against Women," *National NOW Times*, Spring 2008.

Kirk Makin

"Warring Couples Misuse Courts, Judge Says," *Globe & Mail* (Toronto), April 9, 2008.

Anora McGaha

"Stopping Domestic Abuse Before It Starts," *Redbook*, February 2009.

Christina Hoff Sommers

"Persistent Myths in Feminist Scholarship," *Chronicle of Higher Education*, June 29, 2009.

Liz Welch

"Three Generations of Domestic Violence Stop Here," *Glamour*, November 2009.

Cathy Young

"Men's Rights," *Forbes*, November 19, 2009.

What Laws Will Best Reduce Domestic Violence?

Chapter Preface

While most Americans agree that domestic violence is a serious problem that requires intervention, commentators fiercely debate about which institutions should be responsible for addressing domestic violence and about the boundaries of intervention. Some oppose federal involvement and sweeping legislation, preferring state and local laws that focus on keeping the family together. Others, who believe that domestic violence is a widespread problem with social causes, prefer federal involvement and expansive legislation backed by significant funding. For example, while women's groups claim that successful federal programs established under the 1994 Violence Against Women Act (VAWA) should be expanded, others argue that VAWA should be reformed or abandoned altogether.

Those whose objective is to convince Congress to abandon or radically reform VAWA argue that the act, as written, breaks up families and leaves children fatherless. The act, these analysts assert, focuses on separating couples and urging divorce rather than counseling. According to Michael McCormick of the American Coalition for Fathers and Children, VAWA funding supports "a one-sided agenda driven by people who really don't want to see families stay together." In fact, some argue, VAWA is not even about stopping domestic violence. They assert that VAWA promotes a feminist agenda that paints all men as abusers and women as victims. "If proponents were truly concerned about helping victims, they would demand that all intervention and funding be gender neutral and gender inclusive," writes family law attorney Lisa Scott.

While McCormick and Scott believe that the act should be abandoned altogether, some VAWA opponents simply want the act to be gender neutral. According to David Burroughs, legislative counsel for the Safe Homes for Children and Families Coalition, abused men have a hard time finding legal help or access to shelters that receive funding from VAWA. He asserts that of victims who apply for free legal services, 20 percent are men, but they receive less than 1 percent of these services. Moreover, he claims, few domestic violence shelters across the nation are even open to men.

VAWA supporters dispute the claim that the act is not gender neutral. According to Jill Morris of the National Coalition Against Domestic Violence, "Nothing in the act denies services, programs, funding or assistance to male victims of violence." She also disputes the claim that VAWA is not about helping victims. Morris and other VAWA supporters cite statistics on the success of the act. Indeed, in the years since Congress passed VAWA in 1994, domestic violence has dropped more than 50 percent. Before 1994, there was little public debate about the problem. Many believed family violence to be a private matter. Today, however, the issue is out in the open in part due to VAWA and the services it offers, supporters maintain. Nevertheless, VAWA proponents believe that more can be done. For example, according to Lynn Rosenthal of the National Network to End Domestic Violence, 38 percent of domestic violence victims become homeless. "Homelessness does not cause domestic violence, but rather the opposite," Rosenthal claims. She cites the example of a North Carolina woman who was evicted from her apartment because of noise after her ex-boyfriend shot her. Women in these situations need to be protected not only from violence but also from homelessness, VAWA supporters suggest. Expanding VAWA to address homelessness and other problems facing victims of domestic violence, advocates believe, is therefore necessary.

Whether VAWA should be expanded, reformed, or abandoned remains hotly contested by people on both sides of the domestic violence debate. The authors in the following chapter discuss VAWA and other controversies related to domestic violence as they debate the question: What laws will best reduce domestic violence?

> *"Every day, VAWA [Violence Against Women Act] funding makes a difference in how communities across America help victims and hold offenders accountable."*

The Violence Against Women Act Is Necessary to Reduce Domestic Violence

Catherine Pierce

In the following viewpoint, Catherine Pierce asserts that the Violence Against Women Act (VAWA) has done much to reduce domestic violence nationwide. In fact, she maintains, between January and June 2008, more than thirty-five hundred individuals were arrested for protection order violations, and from January 2005 to June 2008, VAWA provided for the training of thousands of law enforcement officers, prosecutors, and court personnel on how best to respond to domestic violence. Pierce reasons, however, that to truly reduce domestic violence, in-

Catherine Pierce, "Statement of Catherine Pierce, Acting Director, Office on Violence Against Women, United States Department of Justice, Before the United States Senate Committee on the Judiciary Hearing Entitled 'The Continued Importance of the Violence Against Women Act,'" Justice.gov, June 10, 2009, pp. 1–3, 6, 8, 11–12. Copyright © 2009 by Justice.gov. All rights reserved. Reproduced by permission.

creased funding will be necessary to train an expanded group of community partners. *Pierce is acting director of the US Department of Justice Office of Violence Against Women.*

As you read, consider the following questions:

1. What has grown more common in the years since VAWA's enactment, according to Pierce?

2. From whom does the author claim domestic violence survivors are more inclined to seek services?

3. What are some of the risk factors associated with increased danger for women in violent relationships, in the author's view?

The Office on Violence Against Women (OVW) administers financial support and technical assistance to communities across the country that are creating programs, policies, and practices aimed at ending domestic violence, dating violence, sexual assault and stalking. Our mission is to provide national leadership to improve the Nation's response to these crimes through the implementation of the Violence Against Women Act [VAWA] of 1994, the Violence Against Women Act of 2000, and the Violence Against Women Act of 2005. OVW pursues this mission by supporting community efforts, enhancing education and training, disseminating promising practices, launching special initiatives, and leading the Nation's efforts to end violence against women.

Responding to Violence Against Women

OVW's grant programs fund a broad spectrum of activities designed to serve victims and hold offenders accountable. . . . These grant programs fund States, local governments, tribal governments, and nonprofit organizations to help communities across America develop innovative strategies to respond to violence against women. With our funding, communities are forging effective partnerships among Federal, State, local and tribal governments, and between the criminal justice system and victim advocates, and are providing much-needed services to victims. Taken together, these programs address a host of different issues that communities face in responding to violence against women, including: the importance of training police, prosecutors, and court personnel; the unique barriers faced by rural communities; the critical need of victims for legal assistance, transitional housing, and supervised visitation services; the special needs of elderly victims and those with disabilities; and the high rate of violence against women in Indian country.

Since 1995, OVW has made grant awards and cooperative agreements totaling over $3.5 billion to communities across the United States.

Making a Difference

Every day, VAWA funding makes a difference in how communities across America help victims and hold offenders accountable. For example, in the six-month reporting period from January to June 2008 alone, OVW discretionary program grantees reported that:

- Nearly 115,500 victims were served;

- More than 228,000 services (including shelter, civil legal assistance and crisis intervention) were provided to victims;

- More than 3,500 individuals were arrested for violation of protection orders; and

- 261,622 protection orders were granted in jurisdictions that receive funding from OVW's Grants to Encourage Arrest Policies and Enforcement of Protection Orders Program (Arrest Program).

In addition, subgrantees receiving funding awarded by States through OVW's STOP Violence Against Women Formula Grant Program (STOP Program) reported that, in calendar year 2007:

- More than 505,000 victims were served;

- Over 1,201,000 services were provided to victims; and

- More than 4,700 individuals were arrested for violations of protection orders.

These funds not only help the victims who receive services; they are used by OVW grantees to change the way that our criminal justice system responds to domestic violence, dating violence, sexual assault, and stalking. Again, the raw numbers show the far reach of VAWA funding:

- During the three-and-a-half year period from January 2005, through June 2008, OVW's grantees reported training nearly 875,000 individuals, including 142,339 law enforcement officers, 15,380 prosecutors, and 24,159 court personnel.

- During the four-year period of 2004 through 2007 combined, STOP subgrantees reported training about 1,138,000 individuals, including 347,382 law enforcement officers, 25,715 prosecutors, and 37,775 court personnel.

We cannot discuss the victims who have been helped with VAWA funds without recognizing the work of the National Domestic Violence Hotline, which was created with funding first authorized by VAWA in 1994 and is administered by the Department of Health and Human Services (HHS). Today, the trained advocates who staff this toll-free hotline answer an average of 21,000 calls a month from victims and their friends and families nationwide. These advocates not only provide immediate crisis counseling but can connect victims with service providers in their local communities.

The Coordinated Community Response

One of the signature achievements of OVW's grant programs is the re-envisioning of the concept of a coordinated community response. When OVW implemented its first VAWA programs, our vision for a successful coordinated community response focused on improving the criminal justice response. We encouraged grantees to bring together law enforcement officers, prosecutors, and non-profit, non-governmental victim advocates to share their experience and use their distinct roles to improve a community-defined response to violence against women. We now recognize that truly effective coordinated community responses must be informed by the experiences of survivors and must be broad enough to include a diverse group of community partners that affect the safety of survivors and the accountability of perpetrators. Community partners should include health care providers, cultural groups, and neighborhood organizations, as well as the criminal and civil justice systems and housing and homeless organizations. This expanded view recognizes that many victims do not report to law enforcement or do not choose to pursue a criminal justice-based response.

In the years since VAWA's enactment, we have witnessed a sea-change in the way that communities respond to violence against women. Communities recognize the specialized needs of victims and the training required to effectively handle domestic violence and sexual assault cases. As a result, dedicated units of law enforcement officers and prosecutors have grown far more common—often with the support of VAWA funds. We have also witnessed and supported the growth of dedicated dockets and courts. Further, we have worked to ensure that communities have opportunities to test innovative practices.

OCTOBER IS DOMESTIC VIOLENCE AWARENESS MONTH

1 IN 4 WOMEN IN THE U.S. WILL EXPERIENCE DOMESTIC VIOLENCE

© 2009 Jeff Parker, Florida Today, and PoliticalCartoons.com.

Expanding Training

Training and technical assistance ensure that professionals have the tools to respond effectively to these crimes. We must continue to support high quality education and training on an ongoing basis, given the high rate of turnover and burn out in this work. OVW works closely with national experts to train, educate, and disseminate promising practices to advocates, clinicians, police, prosecutors, judges, health care practitioners, and many other professionals who are on the front lines. . . .

OVW has launched a number of demonstration projects and special initiatives that test promising practices, address areas of special need, and build capacity in communities. We also have worked with our Federal partners to widen our understanding of the prevalence and nature of violence against women. . . .

While we are rightly proud of our accomplishments over the past fifteen years, we recognize that there is much for us to do in the future. Looking forward, the Office will focus on a number of areas where we know that greater effort is needed. We also plan to enhance our partnership with the National Institute of Justice to ensure that research informs practice and that practice informs research. . . .

OVW feels strongly that the best response to violence against women—the response most likely to empower victims and hold offenders accountable—is a response that is driven and defined by the community served. Research indicates that survivors are more inclined to seek services from organizations that are familiar with their culture, language and background. Culturally specific community-based organizations are more likely to understand the obstacles that victims from their communities face when attempting to access services. These organizations also are better equipped to engage their communities. Whether they serve persons of communities of color, the lesbian/gay/bisexual/transgender community, or the Deaf community, these organizations play a vital role in providing services that are relevant to their communities. . . .

Addressing Domestic Violence Homicide

OVW recognizes the need to focus future efforts on the prevention of domestic violence homicide. Research has identified several risk factors associated with increased danger for women in violent relationships. These include an abuser's threats to kill or harm her, himself, or their children; unemployment; forced sex; and the presence of a gun. Advocates, law enforcement officers, prosecutors, and the courts must take aggressive steps to plan for a victim's safety when any combination of risk factors is present. By the time abuse escalates to homicide, we know that someone in the family, the neighborhood, or the perpetrator's or victim's workplace is aware that something is terribly wrong. OVW will continue to partner with other Federal agencies, the research community, criminal justice organizations, and advocacy groups to develop innovative responses with the hope and intention of preventing future domestic violence homicides.

Research indicates that a victim of domestic violence is more likely to suffer a fatal injury if a firearm is present in her home. For that reason, OVW has recently focused our efforts on the federal firearms provisions that prohibit firearms possession by persons subject to qualified restraining orders and convicted of misdemeanor crimes of domestic violence. For example, in July 2008, we conducted a Washington Metropolitan Summit with Federal, State and local officials to discuss, among other things, effective tools to successfully prosecute domestic violence offenders and to forfeit those firearms involved in domestic violence offenses. In September 2006, we brought together Federal, State, Tribal, and local teams for a National Summit on Firearms and Domestic Violence. At the Summit, the teams were charged with developing strategies to ensure the implementation of the firearms prohibitions. One of the remaining challenges highlighted at the Summit is the issue of the safe storage and proper return of firearms to persons whose protection orders have expired. We will continue to examine these important issues in the future.

> "Reform the Violence Against Women Act (VAWA), make it gender-neutral, and assure men that family courts will accord them constitutional rights."

The Violence Against Women Act Should Be Reformed

Phyllis Schlafly

In the following viewpoint, Phyllis Schlafly argues that Congress should reform the Violence Against Women Act (VAWA). Feminists did not design VAWA to protect women but to promote divorce and hatred of men, she claims. As written, VAWA deprives men of due process protection when faced with allegations of domestic violence. Moreover, Schlafly asserts, VAWA is not gender neutral; it ignores the threat to men who are victims of domestic violence. Reforming VAWA will restore men's civil rights and prevent women from using the act as a tool in divorce proceedings at the expense of men who are presumed guilty without evidence. Phyllis Schlafly, a constitutional lawyer, is a conservative activist and author.

As you read, consider the following questions:

1. What hypocrisy does Schlafly claim VAWA illustrates?

Phyllis Schlafly, "A Good Father's Day Gift," Townhall.com, June 19, 2010. Copyright © 2010 by Townhall.com. All rights reserved. Reproduced by permission of the author.

2. According to the author, what does charging domestic violence practically guarantee?

3. In the author's opinion, how should domestic violence be redefined?

A good Father's Day gift would be to reform the Violence Against Women Act (VAWA), make it gender-neutral, and assure men that family courts will accord them constitutional rights equivalent to those enjoyed by murderers and robbers. VAWA will be coming up for its five-year reauthorization later this year [2010], and that will be the time to hold balanced hearings and eliminate VAWA's discrimination against men.

Not a Gender-Neutral Law

VAWA illustrates the hypocrisy of noisy feminist demands that we kowtow to their ideology of gender neutrality, to their claim that there is no difference between male and female, and to their opposition to stereotyping and gender profiling. VAWA is based on the proposition that there are, indeed, innate gender differences: Men are naturally batterers, and women are naturally victims.

Feminist supporters of VAWA obviously share Jessica Valenti's recent assertion in *The Washington Post* that American women are oppressed by the "patriarchy" and that "it needs to end." One way they hope to end it is by using the extravagantly expensive and discriminatory VAWA, which was passed in 1994 as a payoff to the feminists for helping to elect Bill Clinton president in 1992.

VAWA is not designed to eliminate or punish violence, but to punish only alleged violence against women. Most of the shelters financed by VAWA do not accept men as victims.

A Lack of Accountability

VAWA has been known from the get-go as "feminist pork" because it puts nearly $1 billion a year of U.S. taxpayers' money into the hands of the radical feminists without any accountability for how the money is spent. Feminists have set up shop in shelters where they promote divorce, marriage breakup, hatred of men and false accusations, while rejecting marriage counseling, reconciliation, drug-abuse treatment and evidence of mutual-partner abuse.

Feminists have changed state laws to include a loosey-goosey definition of family violence. It doesn't have to be violent—it can simply be what a man says or how he looks at a woman.

Domestic violence can even be what a woman thinks a man might do or say. Definitions of violence include calling your partner a naughty word, raising your voice, causing "annoyance" or "emotional distress," or just not doing what your partner wants.

VAWA makes taxpayers' money available to the feminists to lobby state legislators to pass feminist laws, to train law enforcement personnel and judges in using those laws, and to fund their enforcement. VAWA provides women with free legal counsel to pursue their allegations while men are left on their own to find and pay a lawyer, or struggle without one.

Feminists have lobbied most states to adopt mandatory-arrest laws, which means that when the police arrive at a disturbance and lack good information on who is to blame, they are nevertheless legally bound to arrest somebody. Three guesses who is usually arrested.

Losing Constitutional Rights

Feminists have lobbied most states to pass no-drop prosecution laws, which require proceeding with prosecution even if the woman recants her charges or wants to drop them. Studies show that women do recant or ask to drop the charges in 60 percent of criminal allegations, but the law requires the man to be prosecuted anyway, which means he loses his constitutional right to confront his accuser.

Needed VAWA Reforms

- Domestic violence is a state matter. Existing Federal laws should be repealed or allowed to expire.

- Domestic violence laws must be gender neutral. . . .

- Domestic violence and abuse laws must not violate the rights to due process and equal protection under the law.

- False allegations of domestic violence . . . must be dealt with as criminal acts.

- Domestic violence laws at all levels of government must exist solely in the criminal codes.

"VAWA: A Four-Letter Word That Means Tyranny,"
Washington Times National Weekly Edition,
July 11 to 17, 2005.

Charging domestic violence practically guarantees that a woman will get custody of the children and sever forever the father's relationship with his children even though the alleged violence had nothing whatever to do with any abuse of the children. Judges are required to consider allegations of domestic violence in awarding child custody, even though no evidence of abuse was ever presented or proven.

It seems elementary that husbands and fathers who are accused by their wives or girlfriends should have the constitutional rights accorded to any criminal, but they are routinely denied equal treatment under law, the right to a fair trial, the presumption of innocence until proven guilty and the right to own a gun. The accusation also destroys his employability, which diminishes her income as well as his.

Based on a woman's unsubstantiated allegations of trivial offenses, family courts deprive thousands of men of their fundamental right to parent their own children. VAWA has a built-in incentive for the woman to make false charges of domestic violence because she knows she will never be prosecuted for perjury.

Domestic violence should be redefined to mean violence. We must eliminate the incentive for false accusations, which includes getting a restraining order as the "gamesmanship" for divorce, child custody, money, and ownership of and access to the family home.

Reforming VAWA is today's basic civil rights issue. All persons accused of domestic violence, men and women, are entitled to have fundamental constitutional rights in court, including due process and the presumption of innocence until proven guilty by clear and convincing evidence.

> *"I'd put people who batter their family members right up there with the mentally ill . . . on the list of people who should never, ever be allowed near a gun."*

Laws Prohibiting Domestic Violence Offenders from Owning Guns Will Reduce Homicides

Ryan Brown

In the following viewpoint, Ryan Brown claims that people who abuse family members should not be able to purchase or possess guns. Indeed, he maintains, Congress passed a law in 1996 that bans abusers from doing so. According to Brown, studies reveal that guns increase the risk by five times of intimate partner homicide. Thus, the author asserts, it came as a surprise that domestic violence activists did not respond when legal experts predicted a flood of challenges to laws following the US Supreme Court ruling that states cannot ban firearm ownership. At the time this viewpoint was written, Brown was an intern at Salon .com.

As you read, consider the following questions:

1. What did Herb Titus of Gun Owners of America claim was first on the organization's slate of issues, according to Brown?

2. How does Brown distinguish a domestic violence misdemeanor from other minor criminal convictions?

3. According to the author, what is a dangerous misstep for women's rights advocates?

Should perpetrators of domestic violence be allowed to own guns?

Now there's a question I never thought I'd have to ask. Call me crazy, but I'd put people who batter their family members right up there with the mentally ill and Dick Cheney[1] on the list of people who should never, ever be allowed near a gun. And Congress agrees; that's why in 1996 it passed a law that barred anyone convicted of misdemeanor domestic violence from transporting, owning or using a gun in this country.

Challenging Gun Bans

But that may be about to change. In a contentious 5–4 decision, the Supreme Court ruled yesterday [June 28, 2010,] that state and local governments cannot enact bans on firearm ownership,[2] and legal experts predict that the ruling will bring a flood of challenges to existing gun control laws—including those that prohibit batterers from owning firearms.

1. In February 2006, then vice president Dick Cheney accidentally shot Texas attorney Harry Whittington while they were quail hunting in Texas.
2. The Supreme Court decided that its interpretation of the Second Amendment applies equally to the states as it does to the federal government. In its earlier opinion striking down a District of Columbia handgun ban, the Supreme Court in *District of Columbia v. Heller* (June 26, 2008) held that the Second Amendment protects an individual's right to possess a firearm for traditionally lawful purposes such as self-defense within the home.

Guns and Domestic Violence

- American women who are killed by their intimate partners are more likely to be killed with guns than by all other methods combined. . . .

- Women are twice as likely to be shot and killed by intimate partners as they are to be murdered by strangers. . . .

- Approximately 700 American women are shot and killed by intimate partners each year. . . .

- In 2002, background checks noting domestic violence misdemeanor convictions and restraining orders kept 22,000 abusers from purchasing firearms.

Women Against Gun Violence.
www.wagv.org.

Herb Titus, counsel for Gun Owners of America, told NPR [National Public Radio] today that challenging the ban on domestic violence offenders will be first on his slate of issues to tackle using the high court's new ruling. It might sound weird to single out people who beat their children and spouses as a minority group in need of having their civil rights protected, but as gun proponents like Titus see it, firearm ownership is not a privilege, it's a constitutionally protected right, and it should not be revoked on the basis of a minor criminal conviction.

Well, it's one thing if your little infraction against the law was shoplifting or failing a breathalyzer exam. But when you are convicted of violently endangering members of your own family—probably habitually, since domestic violence is rarely an isolated event—it makes sense that the law can throw up barriers that make it harder for you to, you know, violently endanger members of your own family.

The Role of Guns in Domestic Violence

And it's not as though we don't know how guns play into the domestic violence equation. Approximately 700 women are shot and killed by their intimate partners each year. In fact, American women are twice as likely to be killed by their partner as a stranger—and guns cause that risk to skyrocket. One study showed that access to firearms increases the risk of partner homicide five-fold.

Yet, despite the evidence that putting guns in the hands of convicted domestic abusers puts their partners at a fatal risk, and despite the fact that the vast majority of domestic violence victims in this country are women, gun control is rarely framed as a feminist issue. Violence against women and gun violence form a Venn diagram[3] with a dangerous and volatile center, but most advocates are still circling in the outer waters. But that could be a dangerous misstep, especially for this particular issue. As the *American Prospect* points out, no women's rights organizations submitted briefs, which are used by parties not involved in the proceedings to supply additional relevant information, to the Supreme Court in this case. To be fair, perhaps they weren't on 24-hour watch for activists charging out to support the gun rights of domestic abusers. But now that the issue is out there, the longer women's rights advocates refrain from stepping into the debate, the more leeway the pro-firearms lobby will have to set the tone of their argument about the "rights" of batterers—and if you ask me, that's a loaded gun just waiting to go off.

---

3. A Venn diagram, often using interconnecting circles, shows hypothetical relations between a finite sets of things, illustrating set relationships in logic.

> "The infamous Lautenberg Amendment, barring possession of firearms from anyone ever convicted of a misdemeanor crime of domestic violence, is a violation of Second Amendment rights."

Laws Prohibiting Misdemeanor Domestic Violence Offenders from Owning Guns Are Unconstitutional

Jeff Knox

In the following viewpoint, Jeff Knox argues that laws barring those convicted of misdemeanor domestic violence from owning guns are unconstitutional. To interfere with constitutionally guaranteed rights, such as the Second Amendment right to possess guns, the government must show a compelling need, he claims. The claim that application of this legal standard is required only for guns possessed for self-defense is problematic, Knox asserts. The Second Amendment includes no such limita-

Jeff Knox, "An End to the Lautenberg Amendment?," firearmscoalition.org, January 7, 2009. Copyright © 2009 by Firearms Coalition. All rights reserved. Reproduced by permission. Text is available at www.FirearmsCoalition.org. To receive The Firearms Coalition's bi-monthly newsletter, The Knox Hard Corps Report, write to PO Box 3313, Manassas, VA 20108.

tion, he reasons, and courts should tread carefully when inter-
preting laws that limit constitutionally guaranteed rights. Knox
is executive director of the Firearms Coalition, a gun rights orga-
nization.

As you read, consider the following questions:

- Why does Knox claim the Seventh Circuit Court ruling is no reason for gun rights advocates to celebrate just yet?

- According to the author, what are the three ways courts can judge an argument?

- What level of scrutiny did the Seventh Circuit Court use in *United States v. Skoien*, according to Knox?

The Federal Court of Appeals for the 7th Circuit recently declared that the infamous Lautenberg Amendment, barring possession of firearms from anyone ever convicted of a misdemeanor crime of domestic violence, is a violation of Second Amendment rights.

That's good news, but don't fire up the band just yet. The actual conclusion of the 7th Circuit panel was not that Lautenberg violates the Second Amendment, but that prosecutors had failed to effectively argue that it does not. Rather than declaring the law unconstitutional and throwing the case out, the court reversed the guilty verdict and sent the case back to the lower court to give federal prosecutors another chance to build a case. Included in the decision are rather detailed instructions explaining what arguments the prosecution needs to make if they wish to prevail. Like a child's game, the court said, "You forgot to say 'Mother may I' so try it again." If prosecutors carefully apply the lessons laid out in the 7th Circuit's order, the case should result in another conviction that would then be upheld on appeal, but even that isn't assured because the court didn't only provide instructions to the prosecution, they also dropped a hint or two for the defense.

The Facts of the Case

The case against the defendant is pretty straightforward. Police went to Steven Skoien's home and in his pickup parked out front they found a freshly killed deer, a shotgun, ammunition, and a lawful deer tag made out in Skoien's name. Skoien admitted that he had been hunting that morning and used the shotgun to kill the deer.

In court Skoien argued that he only possessed the gun for hunting and that denying him the right to arms was a violation of the Second Amendment.

Prosecutors pointed to a comment made in the *Heller*[1] decision to the effect that their decision "should not be taken to cast doubt on longstanding prohibitions on the possession of firearms by felons and the mentally ill." They argued that this should be recognized to include persons prohibited under Lautenberg, and that the government had a compelling need to restrict guns from domestic violence abusers because such abuse is an indicator for future acts of violence.

The three-judge panel of the 7th Circuit rightly pointed out that a person convicted of a domestic violence misdemeanor is not a felon, and concluded that the government's arguments supporting the assertion of a "compelling need" simply were not good enough. The panel also noted that since the defendant claimed to only possess the shotgun for the purpose of hunting and did not assert a self-defense argument, that his claim did not warrant the full protection of the Second Amendment.

---

1. The Supreme Court in the *District of Columbia v. Heller* case held that the Second Amendment protects an individual's right to possess a firearm for traditionally lawful purposes such as self-defense within the home. The majority said that "although we do not undertake an exhaustive historical analysis today of the full scope of the Second Amendment, nothing in our opinion should be taken to cast doubt on longstanding prohibitions on the possession of firearms by felons and the mentally ill, or laws forbidding the carrying of firearms in sensitive places such as schools and government buildings, or laws imposing conditions and qualifications on the commercial sale of arms."

Problematic Positions

All of this is wrapped around two problematic positions taken by the panel:

1. That the dicta [nonbinding judicial opinion in a case] in *Heller* is binding.

2. That cases involving guns possessed for self-defense deserve more protection from the courts than those involving guns possessed for other than defensive purposes.

In the legal system there are three different ways a court can judge an argument. These three different standards are referred to as levels of scrutiny, and they are applied based on the issues being dealt with. The highest and most rigorous of the three is called "Strict Scrutiny" and is applied to matters dealing with fundamental rights. Under strict scrutiny the government must demonstrate a compelling need to interfere with a person's rights and that interference must be narrowly focused to be as minimal as possible to meet the compelling need. At the other end of the spectrum is what is called "Rational Basis." This level of scrutiny is used when fundamental rights are not really an issue. At this level the government need only demonstrate that their rules are reasonable to meet a general need for order. Between these two extremes is "Intermediate Scrutiny." Intermediate scrutiny is applied when there is only limited involvement of civil rights and no direct impact on any fundamental rights. The government must tread carefully around these rights issues and must demonstrate not only a compelling need, but also a careful application so as to show proper respect and consideration for the rights involved.

In the Skoien case, the 7th Circuit concluded that intermediate scrutiny was appropriate because self-defense was not raised as an issue. They also suggested that if the issue of self-defense had been raised, the court would have to move up to a strict scrutiny standard for reviewing the case. This conclusion begs anyone wishing to use the Second Amendment as a legal defense to be sure to invoke the right to arms in a self-defense context and suggests that the court has amended the words "for self defense" to the end of the Second Amendment.

Now prosecutors will no doubt build a case tailored to meeting the court's call for intermediate scrutiny and the defense will assert that Skoien also possessed the shotgun for self-defense purposes and the 7th Circuit will probably get another shot at sorting it all out. By then it is to be hoped that the Supreme Court will have rendered a favorable decision in the *McDonald*[2] case and clarified some of the ambiguity in *Heller.*

2. On June 28, 2010, the Supreme Court, in *McDonald v. Chicago* held that the right of an individual to "keep and bear arms" as protected by the Second Amendment is incorporated by the Due Process Clause of the Fourteenth Amendment and applies to the states.

| "[The International Violence Against Women Act] is . . . distinctive among foreign aid bills in its assertive approach to helping alleviate women's suffering abroad."

The International Violence Against Women Act Helps Women Escape Domestic Violence Worldwide

Elizabeth Weingarten

In the following viewpoint, Elizabeth Weingarten maintains that the International Violence Against Women Act (I-VAWA) was drafted to address the problem of gender violence worldwide by improving the legal and economic status of women as well as their health. Although support for global efforts to end violence against women is significant, she claims, some organizations fear that broad definitions will promote abortion. Still others, Weingarten asserts, worry about the enormous cost of the bill. Supporters nevertheless argue that development-based aid gives women economic power, which leads to improvements in human rights, she concludes. Weingarten is an editorial assistant at the online magazine Slate.

As you read, consider the following questions:

1. What happens when women do not have economic resources, according to Nora O'Connell, as cited by the author?

2. What language in the Senate's version of I-VAWA troubles David Christensen of the Family Research Council, according to Weingarten?

3. Why does Kristen Lord worry about the future of development-based aid bills like I-VAWA, in the author's opinion?

In 2006, Nora O'Connell, vice-president of the non-profit advocacy group Women Thrive, traveled to Markala, a small village in the mountains of Honduras, to learn about the success of an all-female coffee cooperative. The cooperative, Coordinadora de Mujeres Campesinas de La Paz (COMUCAP), trains women to grow and sell coffee and aloe vera. Today, it employs over 256 women in the community.

The Importance of Economic Power

When she asked COMUCAP's founder, Dulce Marlen Contreras, why she started the cooperative, O'Connell recalls, "I was expecting to hear about the challenges they faced in terms of poverty."

Instead, O'Connell and her team learned about the less obvious reason for the organization's genesis: the prevalence of domestic violence in the community. The women, O'Connell says, were mistreated at home. And if they did summon the will to report their husbands' abusive behavior to the police, the municipal government did nothing to help them.

COMUCAP works, O'Connell explains, because it harnesses a basic societal law: economic power leads to social power. "When women don't have economic resources, they are more likely to be trapped in violent situations," O'Connell says. But by earning an income, women gain the comfort of financial independence, and thus the option to pick up and find a better life somewhere else.

O'Connell evokes the story of COMUCAP when explaining why Women Thrive—in conjunction with Amnesty International USA and the Family Violence Prevention Fund—helped develop I-VAWA (S.2982, HR. 4594), or the International Violence Against Women Act. Originally introduced in the House and Senate during the last Congress, the bill was reintroduced in February 2010 by Senators John Kerry (D-Mass.), Barbara Boxer (D-Calif.), Susan Collins (R-Maine) and Olympia Snowe (R-Maine) and Representatives Bill Delahunt (D-Mass.) and Ted Poe (R-Texas). . . .

Helping Victims Worldwide

Given its high-profile congressional backers and [the Barack] Obama administration's emphasis on foreign aid, it seems that I-VAWA may be successful in committee come November [2010]. At last week's [September 2010] Millennium Development Goals Summit at the United Nations, Obama emphasized the importance of the U.S. role in global development and aid—specifically citing women's issues as being vital to international security and economic growth. Toward the end of his speech, Obama appeared to refer indirectly to I-VAWA.

"We know that countries are more likely to prosper when they tap the talents of all their people," he said. "That's why we're investing in the health, education and rights of women, and working to empower the next generation of women entrepreneurs and leaders. Because when mothers and daughters have access to opportunity, economies grow and governance improves."

I-VAWA is also distinctive among foreign aid bills in its as-sertive approach to helping alleviate women's suffering abroad. It promises to address the issue of women's violence along multiple fronts: health, legal, economic, social, and humanitar-ian. It will begin by designing programs for 5–20 countries, all using various best-practice data that the nonprofits involved in the legislation's development have already gathered.

The bill has bipartisan support in the House and Senate, backing from more than 200 U.S. and overseas nongovern-mental organizations, and additional endorsement from the American public: According to a poll by Women Thrive and the Family Violence Prevention Fund this spring, more than 60 percent of Americans believe ending gender-based violence should be a legislative priority. More than 80 percent support I-VAWA.

"This is one of the few foreign policy issues for the Ameri-can people that is really black and white," says O'Connell con-fidently.

But it may not be that simple. Ostensibly, violence against women isn't a partisan issue. But part of the bill has tapped into two issues that are very much a part of partisan politics: foreign aid funding and abortion.

Opposition from Pro-life Advocates

Stephen Colecchi, director of the office of international justice and peace for the U.S. Conference of Catholic Bishops, sup-ports the goals of the legislation, but is worried that the bill's definition of violence against women is overly broad. "We want to be sure that it does not include the possibility of pro-moting changes in abortion law overseas," Colecchi explains.

David Christensen, the senior director of congressional af-fairs at the Family Research Council, shares Colecchi's con-cerns. He points to the definition given for 'violence against women and girls' in the Senate's version of the bill as trouble-some. The bill defines violence against women as "any act of

What I-VAWA Would Do

- Address violence against women and girls comprehensively, by supporting health, legal, economic, social, and humanitarian assistance sectors and incorporating violence prevention and response best practices into such programs.

- Alleviate poverty and increase the cost effectiveness of foreign assistance by investing in women.

- Define a clear mandate for Senior Officials in the Department of State and USAID [US Agency for International Development] for leadership, accountability and coordination in preventing and responding to violence against women and girls.

- Enable the U.S. government to develop a faster and more efficient response to violence against women in humanitarian emergencies and conflict-related situations.

- Build the effectiveness of overseas non-governmental organizations—particularly women's non-governmental organizations—in addressing violence against women.

Amnesty International USA, Family Violence Prevention Fund, and Women Thrive Worldwide, Summer 2010.

violence against women or girls that results in, or is likely to result in, physical, sexual, or psychological harm . . . or arbitrary deprivations of liberty . . ."

"What is 'arbitrary deprivation of liberty'?" asks Christensen. The bill, he says, "seems innocuous," but "has some serious problems in it." For example, "If you believe abortion is an inherent right and you're in a country that does not allow abortion, then this potentially could be interpreted that pro-life law is depriving somebody's liberty."

Another potential problem: I-VAWA doesn't amend the Foreign Assistance Act [FAA]. This, he says, means it isn't covered under the Helms amendment, which states that federal funds can't be used to fund abortion overseas as a method of family planning.

Concerns About the Definition

But a congressional aide at the Senate Foreign Relations Committee who spoke on the condition of anonymity says that the restrictions on foreign assistance, including Helms, apply without needing to amend the FAA. The aide also responded to concerns over the definition of 'violence against women.'

"I-VAWA is not aimed at creating a new definition of 'violence against women,' but rather uses the extremely widely accepted definition put forward in the UNGA [UN General Assembly]," the aide said. "The definition is meant to be a guide, and it does not aim to define every term, the way a criminal statute would."

Despite these claims, Senator Bob Corker (R-Tenn.), a member of the Senate Foreign Relations Committee, says he would oppose the bill in its current form.

"The bill is inconsistent with long-standing U.S. foreign aid policies regarding the sanctity of life," Corker said. "We strongly support much of what is in this legislation and believe it should become law, so hopefully before the bill is brought up again, the necessary changes will be made and the bill can win broad consensus among the committee."

Fears About the Price Tag

Senator Richard Lugar (R-Ind.), the ranking member of the Senate Foreign Relations Committee, thinks some senators will propose amendments to change the bill's language so it can't be misconstrued as pro-abortion. But he'll likely oppose the bill for another reason. "There is no money to pay for it," Lugar says. "This is simply another program that will cost over a billion dollars, and there's nothing provided for it."

I-VAWA is an authorization bill, which means it doesn't actually provide any funding. If passed, I-VAWA will be included in a springtime appropriations bill which would actually fund the legislation's programs. According to a congressional aide in the Senate Foreign Relations Committee and a staffer at one of the nonprofit organizations that helped draft the bill, Senator Lugar referenced an outdated and incorrect price tag: The price of the legislation will not be over a billion dollars. And since they are still unclear about how many countries will be included in the pilot program (as few as 5, as many as 20), it's impossible to assign a specific dollar amount to the bill.

The typical U.S. International Affairs budget hovers around $55 billion each fiscal year (FY). Anda Adams, the associate director for the Brookings Institution Center for Universal Education, says that number rose to $58.94 billion in 2010 because of a supplemental bill passed to fund activities in Afghanistan, Iraq, and Haiti. The House has request[ed] $54 billion for FY11, and the Senate has requested $56 billion.

That outcome would be especially likely if Democrats lose seats in the upcoming election. I-VAWA's fate will be determined by how willing the next Congress will be to allocate funds to foreign aid. Some experts are cheering a recent poll from the USGLC [US Global Leadership Coalition], which reveals support among military personnel for diplomacy and development-based aid. Some experts say the poll could help convince Congress to allocate more funds to development-based aid, given the credibility that military personnel tend to have among legislators.

Others, such as Kristen Lord, the vice president and director of studies at the Center for a New American Security, worry about the future of development-based aid bills like I-VAWA.

"My concern is we haven't seen very much movement in Congress investing more money in diplomacy and development," she says, citing the "all-star" team in the Obama administration—[US Secretary of State Hillary] Clinton, [Chairman of the Joint Chiefs of Staff Admiral Mike] Mullen and [US Secretary of Defense Robert] Gates—supporting this legislation. "Sometimes I worry that if this team can't pull this off, if they can't address this balance, what does that portend for the future?"

VIEWPOINT 6

"The [International Violence Against Women Act] . . . is a thinly-veiled push for anti-family policies."

The International Violence Against Women Act Destroys Families

Janice Shaw Crouse

In the following viewpoint, Janice Shaw Crouse maintains that the International Violence Against Women Act (I-VAWA) will promote feminist antifamily policies on a global scale. The break-down of marriage and family, however, is what increases domestic violence, she argues. The United Nations has interpreted broad definitions of violence to include being denied access to abortion services, Crouse claims. Moreover, she asserts, these broad definitions encourage false accusations that break up fami-lies and promote welfare dependence. Crouse, a former speech-writer for President George H.W. Bush, is a political commenta-tor for Concerned Women for America, a conservative women's organization.

Janice Shaw Crouse, "Anti-violence Bill Promotes Abortion and Gender Quotas," Townhall.com, September 27, 2010. Copyright © 2010 by Townhall.com. All rights reserved. Reproduced by permission of the author, a member of Concerned Women for America Legislative Action Committee.

As you read, consider the following questions:

1. Where are the problems with I-VAWA hidden, in Crouse's opinion?

2. According to the author, where is the safest and most nurturing place for the nation's women and children?

3. In the author's view, what can the loose term *gender-based violence* mean?

This week [September 2010] the Senate Foreign Relations Committee will begin addressing the proposed International Violence Against Women Act (I-VAWA)—S. 2982 and H.R. 4594. With a price tag of over $1 billion over the next five years, the bill will add to the hodge-podge collection of "progressive" initiatives that are pushing the U.S. to the brink of financial crisis. Feminist groups are pushing action on the legislation before the November elections—for obvious reasons. Like so many feminist proposals, the rhetoric sounds great. Is there anybody, other than the jihadists, who is not opposed to violence against women? The problems with I-VAWA are hidden in the fine print under the lofty rhetoric; the agenda is predictable: anything promoting so-called "women's rights" is a thinly-veiled push for anti-family policies, gender quotas, and, of course, abortion-on-demand, all on a global scale.

Promoting Hidden Agendas

The issue of violence against women has a sketchy past, where facts are obscured by emotional accounts of battering and other violence. Any normal person is appalled anytime a stronger person takes advantage of or abuses a more vulnerable person. Decent people are outraged at real abuse, but false accusations and trumped up campaigns to promote hidden agendas are equally outrageous. By now, everybody knows that the old 1993 story about violent attacks on women increasing on Super Bowl Sunday was false; the "study" was debunked just days after it first appeared. Even so, periodically the "fact" still gets reported as truth. By now, everybody should also know that the majority of "domestic violence" incidences are committed by the boyfriends of mothers, not husbands and biological fathers. Sadly, however, statistics are now kept on "intimate partner" violence, and we refer to "domestic abuse" rather than breaking the violence into types of intimate partners (whether a husband, former husband, or boyfriend) or domestic household arrangement (whether marriage or cohabitation).

The facts are clear: the breakdown of marriage and family has been a major factor in increasing violence and abuse against women and children. The sad reality is that we are spinning our wheels as a nation in trying to keep up with the problems of women who are not protected by their husbands and of children who are denied the presence and protection of mature, concerned fathers. How many more women and children will be abused before we acknowledge that the investment America needs to make for the nation's women and children is to encourage and support marriage? A married father-mother home is the safest and most nurturing place for the nation's women and children.

The Link to Reproductive Rights

Further, the urban myths continue alongside the long-standing practice of feminists equating a lack of "reproductive services" with "domestic violence." The I-VAWA (Section 3) acknowledges U.N. Security Council Resolution 1325—which, as those who are knowledgeable about the U.N. recognize, is the section that is cited as mandating the protection of reproductive rights. The I-VAWA would allocate $10 million a year to the United Nations Development Fund for Women, UNIFEM[1] (Section 201), one of the major U.N. agencies devoted to promoting the Millennium Development Goals (MDGs), which prominently feature reproductive and gender rights. First, note that the UNIFEM definition of domestic violence includes "psychological violence perpetrated or condoned by the government of the country in which the victim is a resident" (Section 4). Second, what the American public needs to be aware of is that the U.N.'s interpretation of "psychological violence" includes "mental distress" brought on by lack of access to abortion services.

Plus, the money trail is a maze of symbiotic relationships. For instance, the I-VAWA bill (Section 112) includes provisions for grants to Women's Nongovernmental Organizations and Community-Based Organizations. The organization that has taken the lead in promoting I-VAWA is the Family Violence Prevention Fund (FVPF), "which stands to receive a major portion of I-VAWA funds." The FVPF promotes "training and sensitization" programs for judges and judicial officials that will solidify "access to reproductive services."

Other concerns regarding I-VAWA are equally troubling. The broad definitions of "violence" and the use of terms like "psychological harm" and "coercion" leave plenty of room for false accusations of abuse that will break up families and increase welfare dependence. The bill establishes an "Ambassador-at-Large for Global Women's Issues"—what some have called a "feminist czar" (Section 101) that would establish powers under one person's control that would supersede current and established policy-making and financial procedures.

Ironically and unbelievably, the I-VAWA does not address sex-selective abortion, which is one of today's most egregious policies perpetuating violence against women. Both China and India are facing shortages of marriageable-age women as a re-

1. UNIFEM has since been dissolved and incorporated into the newly established UN Entity for Gender Equality and Empowerment of Women (UN Women).

sult of decades of this practice, a demographic fact that has sociologists and politicians concerned about the future of those nations.

The I-VAWA is promoted as a "groundbreaking bill" that will "apply the force of U.S. diplomacy and foreign assistance to preventing gender-based violence." That loose term—gender-based violence—can mean anything and generally covers a wide range of ideological goals from the "women's rights" agenda. In the U.S., the bill will seek to "change public attitudes" and "social norms," efforts that are potentially "biased in their content and ideological in their purpose."

Though these vague, nebulous goals are dressed up to sound wonderful and disguise the intent of the ideologues who promote them, their meaning can be as misleading—and disastrous—as the campaign slogan of "hope" and "change."

> "When almost any action can be construed as 'abusive' and an allegation becomes essentially irrefutable, we have reached the point of criminalizing everyday partner interactions."

Criminalizing Partner Discord Hurts True Domestic Violence Victims

Stop Abusive and Violent Environments

In the following viewpoint, Stop Abuse and Violent Environments (SAVE) asserts that broad definitions of domestic violence turn family discord into a crime. As a result, SAVE claims, poorly crafted laws that define violence as "getting annoyed if the victim disagrees" break families apart. Moreover, broad interpretations of coercion for some might include attempts to tell a partner what to wear or what channel to watch, SAVE maintains. Criminalizing the disagreements that make up everyday life overburdens the criminal justice system, making it more difficult for the system to help true victims, the organization reasons. SAVE is an organization that promotes fathers' rights.

As you read, consider the following questions:

1. According to SAVE, what set the stage for a dramatic broadening of statutory definitions of domestic violence at the state level?

2. According to the author, what do most people typically think of when they hear the word "violence"?

3. How many jurisdictions have broadened their civil definition of domestic violence, according to SAVE?

In 1780, John Adams of Massachusetts advanced the notion that the fledgling American democracy should be a "government of laws and not of men." Indeed, rule of law is considered to be a prerequisite to democracy because it promotes fairness and justice.

Rule of law rests on the notion that legal offenses must be defined by concrete actions and verifiable harms, are enforceable by law enforcement personnel, and are amenable to judicial confirmation or refutation. Traditional Anglo-American notions of a crime require both a guilty act (referred to as "actus reus") and guilty intention ("mens rea").

The original Family Violence Prevention and Service Act (FVPSA) incorporated this definition of family violence:

> The term "family violence" means any act or threatened act of violence, including any forceful detention of an individual, which—
>
> (A) results or threatens to result in physical injury;

In contrast, the Violence Against Women Act [VAWA] relies on a broader definition: "The term 'domestic violence' *includes* felony or misdemeanor crimes of violence."

VAWA's use of the open-ended word "includes" set the stage for a dramatic broadening of statutory definitions of domestic violence at the state level. From 1997 to 2003, it is estimated that states enacted 1,500 new domestic violence laws, an average of 30 per state over the 7-year period.

Drawing Attention to the Problem

In New Mexico, revamped abuse laws set the stage for this nationally publicized incident:

> On December 15, 2005, Santa Fe District Court Judge Daniel Sanchez issued a temporary restraining order to protect Colleen Nestler. According to Nestler, for the past 11 years a man had been sending her unwanted coded messages over the airwaves expressing his desire to marry her. Her alleged harasser: CBS talk show host David Letterman.

> Later asked to explain why he had issued a restraining order on the basis of such an unusual complaint, Judge Sanchez answered that Ms. Nestler had filled out the restraining order request form correctly. The order was later dropped.

This [viewpoint] traces the broadening definitions of "domestic violence" in state-level civil laws over the last 25 years, analyzes contemporary efforts to further expand definitions, and examines the effects of such trends.

What Makes a Relationship "Domestic"?

The first question involves the "who" of domestic violence. The original Violence Against Women Act of 1994 was restricted to only married and co-habiting couples. . . .

But the 2000 reauthorization of the Violence Against Women Act broadened the "who" to encompass dating couples. This notion is now reflected in many state laws. In Rhode Island, for example, persons who "are or have been in a substantive *dating or engagement relationship* within the past one year" are considered to be governed by the state's domestic abuse statute.

More recently, a number of states have broadened the definition of "domestic" beyond relationships that are intimate or even romantic in nature. . . .

What Actions Represent "Violence"?

When persons hear the word "violence," they typically think of a physical assault that causes an injury, a notion that is consistent with the definition in the Family Violence Prevention and Services Act. This concept continues to be reflected in the laws of several states. For example, the South Carolina law defines abuse simply as:

- Physical harm, bodily injury, assault, or the threat of physical harm

- Sexual criminal offenses committed against a family or household member by a family or household member

But South Carolina is one of only five states that has limited its definition to physical actions or threats. In the other states, the concept of domestic "violence" has become broader.

The most common strategy has been to define violence in terms of its alleged psychological impact. This is done both by expanding the definition of physical assault to include emotional distress, and by establishing new categories of offenses that are defined in large part by their psychological impact, such as harassment and stalking. . . .

Overall, 46 jurisdictions in the country have broadened their civil definition to include fear, emotional distress, harassment, stalking, or other psychological states. In five states—Alaska, Michigan, New Hampshire, New Mexico, and North Carolina—statutes have all three types of problematic definitions.

In only five states—Connecticut, Kansas, Idaho, Nebraska, and South Carolina—do statutes define domestic violence simply in terms of overt actions that can be objectively proven or refuted in a court of law.

Indistinguishable from Everyday Activities

Despite existing concerns about overly broad definitions of domestic violence, efforts are under way to further expand the construct.

The National Victim Assistance Academy, supported by funds from the Department of Justice, has listed "extreme jealousy and possessiveness" and ignoring, dismissing, or ridiculing the victims' needs as examples of domestic violence.

The U.S. Centers for Disease Control has published a list of actions that it asserts to be examples of intimate partner violence, including "getting annoyed if the victim disagrees," "withholding information from the victim," and "disregarding what the victim wants." . . .

The Office of Violence Against Women presents this definition as a domestic violence "fact:"

> What is Domestic Violence? Domestic violence can be defined as a pattern of abusive behavior in any relationship that is used by one partner to *gain or maintain power and control* over another intimate partner. [emphasis added]

The proposed renewal of the Family Violence Prevention and Services Act includes a similar concept:

> For the purposes of this chapter, the terms 'domestic violence and family violence' means any act or pattern of acts of violence, harassment, *coercion*, forcible detention, kidnapping, or abuse. [emphasis added]

It should be noted that the word "coercion" is not defined in the proposed law. So if a person attempts to persuade a partner about where to go for dinner, what TV channel to watch, or what clothes to wear, such actions could be construed as coercive.

Such "offenses" have become indistinguishable from persons' everyday activities of life.

David Letterman's Domestic Violence

This [viewpoint discusses] an account of a restraining order involving David Letterman and Colleen Nestler, a woman he had never met and who lived thousands of miles away. Under state law, how could this incident have possibly occurred?

In New Mexico, the statutory definition of domestic violence includes any of the following actions:

Section 40-13-2: "Any incident by a household member against another household member resulting in ... (2) *severe emotional distress* ... (9) *stalking*, ... [or] (10) *harassment*."

Colleen Nestler claimed that she was suffering from exhaustion and had gone bankrupt over the incident—events that would certainly qualify as "severe emotional distress."

But Mr. Letterman wasn't a member of Colleen Nestler's household. Or was he? According to state law, a household member includes "a spouse, former spouse, family member, including a relative, parent, present or former stepparent, present or former in-law, child or co-parent of a child, *or a person with whom the petitioner has had a continuing personal relationship.*"

According to the petition, Letterman had sent Ms. Nestler telepathic messages for 11 years, which arguably qualifies as a "continuing" relationship. That makes Letterman a household member. So under New Mexico state law, David Letterman engaged in domestic violence against Colleen Nestler, a woman he had never met, seen, or heard of.

Criminalizing Partner Discord

The rule of law is a cornerstone of American democracy. Rule of law helps ensure that true victims are protected, offenders are punished, and justice is served. . . .

Domestic violence laws have defined domestic violence in increasingly broader—and more elusive—terms. In many states, domestic violence is now defined in expansive and essentially limitless terms such as "annoyance," "fear," or even "any other conduct." Some groups are working to expand definitions even farther to encompass the constructs of "power and control," an effort that defies comprehension by traditional legal norms.

When almost any action can be construed as "abusive" and an allegation becomes essentially irrefutable, we have reached the point of criminalizing everyday partner interactions. What remains is an over-extended criminal justice system that finds itself incapable of helping the true victims.

| "*Violence against women is a public scourge, but respecting survivors' wishes must be paramount.*"

Mandatory Arrest Provisions Hurt Some Domestic Violence Victims

Ann Friedman

In the following viewpoint, Ann Friedman argues that, although protecting women from violence is an important goal, good laws also should respect the rights of victims. The mandatory arrest provision of the Violence Against Women Act (VAWA) was included because many police officers were reluctant to arrest batterers, and survivors were reluctant to charge abusers with a crime, she maintains. This broad policy, however, ignores the wishes of some domestic violence victims, Friedman claims. While the goals are admirable, broad laws are not always the answer, particularly in some cases of domestic violence, she reasons. Friedman, a writer and editor, regularly contributes to the American Prospect.

As you read, consider the following questions:

1. What are some of the headlines that made domestic violence a front-page story, according to Friedman?

2. What did the "pro-arrest" policy of the 2005 VAWA disregard, in the author's opinion?

3. In the author's view, what should be the focus of the 2010 reauthorization of VAWA?

This year, violence against women—an issue doggedly championed by feminists but rarely a front-page story—seemed to make headlines in every section of the newspaper. Sports: A hotel worker accused Pittsburgh Steelers quarterback Ben Roethlisberger of raping her. Entertainment: Singer Chris Brown was sentenced to probation for assaulting his girlfriend and fellow hip-hop star, Rihanna. International: After decades on the lam, Roman Polanski was arrested in Switzerland for drugging and raping a 13-year-old girl in 1977. Politics: Recently seated Sen. Al Franken introduced an amendment to withhold defense contracts from companies like KBR if they prevent their employees from speaking out about sexual assault. And the health-reform debate revealed that many insurance companies classify domestic violence as a "pre-existing condition," denying coverage to victims of abuse.

The Department of Justice also announced new data on violence against women. Between 1993 and 2008, overall rates of domestic violence and sexual assault dropped, but violence against women is still at epidemic levels. Of every 1,000 American women, 4.3 have experienced domestic abuse, and 89,000 women reported being raped last year. The statistics were released this fall, which also marked the 15th anniversary of the Violence Against Women Act. VAWA, the primary way the federal government addresses this issue, provides funding for domestic-violence shelters, law-enforcement training programs, and services for sexual-assault survivors. While its

Ignoring Victims' Wishes

Many believe mandatory arrest policies disempower victims and diminish their autonomy. . . .

Indeed in many cases the victim does not want the offender to be arrested; he or she just wants to stabilize the situation. Two surveys of abused women reveal higher satisfaction with police actions when the officers complied with the victim's request that they not arrest the alleged offender.

Cases have been documented in which victims become caught up in a rigid criminal justice system that downplays their wishes . . . [for example:]

Following an incident of mutual pushing and shoving, one woman recounted, "I called 911 to prevent the situation from escalating. Thus began the spiral into hell . . . the police told my husband that one of us would have to go to jail. . . . My right to choose was taken away from me and I have been placed in the stereotype of a weak woman with no backbone . . . I am bitter and angry and truly feel like a victim, not of my husband, but of the legal system!"

Stop Abusive and Violent Environments,
Arrest Policies for Domestic Violence, *November 2010.*

goals seem hard to disagree with—protecting women and deterring assault and abuse—the law remains controversial among conservatives who argue it is sexist against men (even though VAWA provides funding for services for men, too, despite the fact that women are five times more likely than men to be victims of domestic violence).

VAWA is also controversial among some liberals but for a very different reason. While overall the legislation has been incredibly successful at increasing privacy protections for survivors and funding the organizations that serve them, VAWA also injects our flawed criminal-justice system into personal relationships. In doing so, it poses a deep quandary for those of us who are critical of that system but believe strongly that rapists and domestic abusers should be accountable for their actions.

Originally, the legislation required states receiving VAWA funds to implement "mandatory arrest" policies if police were called to a home on reports of domestic violence. As Elizabeth M. Schneider writes in her book *Battered Women and Feminist Lawmaking*, the provision was lawmakers' answer to the fact that many police officers are reluctant to arrest batterers—and that many survivors of abuse are reluctant to charge their abusers with a crime. This policy, which was ratcheted down from "mandatory arrest" to "pro-arrest" when VAWA was reauthorized in 2005, disregarded the fact that not all women interact with the criminal-justice system in the same way. An upper-middle-class white woman may conclude that involving the police (getting a restraining order, perhaps) against her abusive husband will make her safer, but will a woman of color in a low-income neighborhood come to the same conclusion? When your community has a contentious history with law enforcement, involving police might not seem like such a good idea.

It's understandable, given the prevalence of violence against women in this country, to want to push for big, systemic solutions to the problem. That is the premise on which VAWA was based. But the deeply personal nature of this crime is what makes such a broad response inherently problematic. Many observers were shocked when Rihanna chose not to press charges against Brown. The woman who, as a child, was raped by Polanski later said that she wished prosecutors would drop the case. This may be hard to accept for those of us who saw the photos of Rihanna's bruised face or read the damning testimony from Polanski's trial, but these women have a right to decline to get involved with the justice system. Violence against women is a public scourge, but respecting survivors' wishes must be paramount.

If our goal is to keep women safe from violence and, failing that, help those who have experienced it to heal and move on, a more personal response may be warranted. Of course, VAWA does fund many programs that do just that. It has funneled grant money to organizations, advocates, and shelters that do critical work within communities to reduce the incidence of violence against women and to support survivors. When it comes time to reauthorize the legislation next year, that's where we should put the focus—on educating men and empowering women.

Periodical and Internet Sources Bibliography

The following articles have been selected to supplement the diverse views presented in this chapter.

Carrie M. Carretta   "Domestic Violence: A Worldwide Exploration," *Journal of Psychological Nursing*, 2008.

Merrill Cousin and Nan Stoops   "Time to Disarm Violent Domestic Abusers," *Seattle Times*, June 15, 2009.

Brenton T. Culpepper   "Missed Opportunity: Congress's Attempted Response to the World's Demand for the Violence Against Women Act," *Vanderbilt Journal of Transnational Law*, 2010.

John L. Esposito and Sheila B. Lalwani   "Domestic Violence: A Global Problem, Not a Religious One," *Los Angeles Times*, October 31, 2010.

Emily Jane Goodman   "Batterers, Their Victims and the Right to Confront Witnesses," *Gotham Gazette*, April 30, 2008.

Tzili Mor   "U.S. Global Duty: To Deter Violence Against Women," *Peace and Freedom*, Fall 2008.

Barack Obama   "Remarks on Domestic Violence Prevention," *Daily Compilation of Presidential Documents*, October 2010.

Carey Roberts   "Yippee, We're All Abusers Now!" Daily Caller, December 7, 2010. www.dailycaller.com.

Ritu Shama   "A Business Case to End Violence Against Women," *Business Week*, October 6, 2010.

Washington Post   "Preemptive Strike: Domestic Violence Suspects Should Be Forced to Relinquish Their Weapons," February 28, 2009.

For Further Discussion

Chapter 1

1. The American College of Obstetricians and Gynecologists argues that domestic violence is a serious national health problem. Stephen Baskerville claims that the statistics on domestic abuse are inflated because they are based on allegations of abuse, not actual crimes. Baskerville argues that lawyers encourage women to make false allegations to gain custody or marital property. Note the affiliation of each viewpoint's author. Does the author's affiliation influence the viewpoint's persuasiveness? Explain why or why not.

2. Mark Mahnkey maintains that men are just as likely to be victims of domestic violence as are women. Elsie Hambrook disputes this claim, arguing that women are much more likely to be victims. The authors both cite studies and statistics to support their views. Which evidence do you find more persuasive? How does each author define "violence"? Do the definitions influence how the evidence should be interpreted? Why or why not?

3. Carrie Mulford and Peggy C. Giordano assert that teen dating violence is a serious problem. Mike Males claims that the interpretation of teen dating violence data is flawed, citing several exaggeration techniques. Do Mulford and Giordano use any of these exaggeration techniques in their viewpoint? Do you think Males would object to their interpretation? Explain your answers.

4. What rhetorical strategy do Humaira Shahid and Ritu Sharma use to support their claim that domestic violence is a global problem that warrants political action? Do you find this strategy persuasive? Explain.

5. The editors of *Information Week* claim that the use of technology by abusers is growing. Do you think the tools the authors recommend will be adequate to address the problem? Explain.

Chapter 2

1. Authors of the viewpoints in this chapter explore several causes of domestic violence. Which cause do you think contributes most to the problem of domestic violence? Explain.

2. How does each author's view about what causes domestic violence inform the strategy that each claims will best address the problem?

3. List each author, his or her occupation and/or affiliation(s), and his or her view on what causes domestic violence. How does the author's affiliation inform his or her point of view? Does this make his or her view more or less persuasive? Explain why or why not, citing each viewpoint.

Chapter 3

1. The National Child Abuse Coalition argues that child protection services (CPS) help protect children from abuse. The National Coalition for Child Protection Reform (NCCPR) claims that CPS actually hurts children because they can remove children from the home based on false allegations and put kids into a foster care system that offers little or no safety. NCCPR claims that inexperienced and overworked caseworkers are partly to blame. If Congress were to increase funding to CPS, as requested by the National Child Abuse Coalition, do you think this would satisfy NCCPR's concerns about child safety? Explain why or why not.

2. Diane L. Rosenfeld believes that restraining orders enhanced by global positioning system (GPS) monitoring will help protect victims from their abusers. Gregory A. Hession claims that because there is no penalty for false allegations, restraining orders are used to gain the advantage in custody proceedings, not to protect victims of abuse. What types of evidence does each author use to support his or her viewpoint? Does the way in which each author defines "victim" influence the persuasiveness of his or her view? Explain.

3. What commonalities among the viewpoints on both sides of the debate can you find in this chapter? Explain, citing examples from the viewpoints.

Chapter 4

1. Catherine Pierce argues that the Violence Against Women Act (VAWA) has effectively reduced domestic violence and, with continued funding, more can be done. Phyllis Schlafly believes VAWA deprives men of due process and should therefore be reformed. What evidence do the authors provide to support their claims? What evidence do you find most persuasive? Explain.

2. Ryan Brown believes that because guns increase the risk of domestic violence homicide, those convicted of domestic violence should not be allowed to purchase or possess guns. Jeff Knox argues that any law that will interfere with the Second Amendment right to purchase and possess a gun must be narrowly focused to meet a compelling need. Do you think reducing the risk of domestic violence homicide is a compelling need? How should a law be written to meet Knox's explanation of "strict scrutiny"?

3. Elizabeth Weingarten argues that the International Violence Against Women Act (I-VAWA) will improve the legal and economic status of women, which will in turn reduce gender violence worldwide. Janice Shaw Crouse argues

that the goals of I-VAWA are not to reduce domestic violence but to promote abortion and expand feminist anti-family policies across the globe. How does the rhetoric of each author differ? Which rhetorical strategy do you find more persuasive? Explain.

4. Stop Abusive and Violent Environments argues that the definitions of domestic violence have become so broad that even family spats are labeled domestic violence. Criminalizing family disagreements, the organization claims, makes it difficult for an already overburdened criminal justice system to help true victims of abuse. Ann Friedman opposes mandatory arrest because it sometimes ignores the needs and wishes of victims. What role does each author believe the criminal justice system should play? How does this influence the author's rhetoric? Explain.

5. What commonalities can you find among the viewpoints on both sides of the debates in the chapter? Citing from the viewpoints, explain your answer.

Organizations to Contact

The editors have compiled the following list of organizations concerned with the issues debated in this book. The descriptions are derived from materials provided by the organizations. All have publications or information available for interested readers. The list was compiled on the date of publication of the present volume; the information provided here may change. Be aware that many organizations take several weeks or longer to respond to inquiries, so allow as much time as possible.

American Academy of Child and Adolescent Psychiatry (AACAP)

3615 Wisconsin Ave. NW, Washington, DC   20016-3007
(202) 966-7300 • fax: (202) 966-2891
website: www.aacap.org

The American Academy of Child and Adolescent Psychiatry is a nonprofit organization that supports and advances child and adolescent psychiatry through research and information distribution. The academy's goal is to provide information that will remove the stigma associated with mental illnesses and ensure proper treatment for children who suffer from mental or behavioral disorders due to child abuse, molestation, or other factors. AACAP publishes Facts for Families, a series that covers a variety of issues concerning disorders that may affect children and adolescents, including domestic abuse.

American Coalition for Fathers and Children (ACFC)

1718 M St. NW, Suite 187, Washington, DC   20036
(800) 978-3237 • fax: (703) 433-9023
e-mail: info@acfc.org
website: www.acfc.org

The American Coalition for Fathers and Children supports efforts to create a family law system that promotes equal rights for all parties affected by divorce and the breakup of a family.

The coalition believes that the Violence Against Women Act destroys families and funds an anti-male, pro-feminist ideological agenda. ACFC publishes the quarterly newspaper the *Liberator*, articles from which are available on its website.

Break the Cycle

5777 W. Century Blvd., Suite 1150, Los Angeles, CA   90045

(310) 286-3383 • fax: (310) 286-3386

website: www.breakthecycle.org

Break the Cycle is a national nonprofit advocacy organization formed to address teen dating violence. The organization believes everyone has the right to safe and healthy relationships, and its mission is to educate and empower youth to build lives and communities free from dating violence and domestic abuse. Break the Cycle asserts that teen dating violence is an urgent, underreported epidemic. On its website the organization provides links to videos and newspaper articles about teen dating violence.

Centers for Disease Control and Prevention—National Center for Injury Prevention and Control (NCIPC)

4770 Buford Hwy. NE, MS F-63, Atlanta, GA   30341-3717

(800) 232-4636

e-mail: cdcinfo@cdc.gov

website: www.cdc.gov/injury

The Centers for Disease Control and Prevention, a part of the US Department of Health and Human Services, includes the National Center for Injury Prevention and Control. The mission of NCIPC is to prevent injuries and violence and reduce their consequences. The NCIPC website provides access to online publications concerning intimate partner violence, including reports such as *World Report on Violence and Health*, as well as fact sheets such as "Understanding Intimate Partner Violence" and "Understanding Teen Dating Violence."

Futures Without Violence

100 Montgomery St., The Presidio, San Francisco, CA   94129
(415) 678-5500 • fax: (415) 252-8991
e-mail: info@futureswithoutviolence.org
website: www.futureswithoutviolence.org

Formerly known as the Family Violence Prevention Fund, Futures Without Violence works to prevent violence within the home and community. It sponsors special education campaigns and was instrumental in lobbying Congress to enact the Violence Against Women Act. On its website, the organization publishes fact sheets, news briefs, and links to articles about domestic violence, including "Post-traumatic Childhood" and "Seven Easy Ways That Every Father Can Matter."

Men Stopping Violence

2785 Lawrenceville Hwy., Suite 112, Decatur, GA   30033
(404) 270-9894 • fax: (404) 270-9895
website: www.menstoppingviolence.org

Men Stopping Violence works locally, nationally, and internationally to change belief systems, social structures, and institutional practices that oppress women and children and dehumanize men. The organization believes that all forms of oppression are interconnected and that efforts to change attitudes in the areas of race, class, gender, age, and sexual orientation are therefore needed to end violence against women. On its website, the organization publishes articles about domestic violence, including "Deconstructing Male Violence" and "Violence Against Women Also a Man's Problem."

Miles Foundation

PO Box 423, Newtown, CT   06470-0423
(203) 270-7861
e-mail: milesfdn@aol.com
website: www.wecaretoo.com/organizations/CT/mF.html

The Miles Foundation is a private nonprofit organization providing comprehensive services to victims of violence associated with the military. The foundation furnishes professional education and training to civilian community-based service providers and military personnel, conducts research, and serves as a resource center for policy makers, advocates, journalists, scholars, researchers, and students. It also fosters administrative and legislative initiatives to improve the military response to domestic violence.

National Coalition Against Domestic Violence (NCADV)
One Broadway, Suite B210, Denver, CO   80203
(303) 839-1852 • fax: (303) 831-9251
website: www.ncadv.org

The National Coalition Against Domestic Violence believes that violence against women and children results from the use of force or threat to achieve and maintain control over others in intimate relationships. The coalition also believes that the abuses of power in society foster battering by perpetuating conditions that condone violence against women and children. NCADV therefore works to change these societal conditions. The coalition publishes fact sheets and a suggested reading list, which are available on its website. Its newsletter, the *Grassroots Connection*, and the *Voice: A Journal of the Battered Women's Movement*, are available with membership.

National Criminal Justice Reference Service (NCJRS)
PO Box 6000, Rockville, MD   20849-6000
(800) 851-3420 • fax: (301) 519-5212
e-mail: askncjrs@ncjrs.gov
website: www.ncjrs.gov

The National Criminal Justice Reference Service is an agency of the US Department of Justice established to prevent and reduce crime and to improve the criminal justice system. The NCJRS website provides access to numerous reports on crime and justice that can be accessed through its search engine or its subject index. Available reports include *Men Who Murder Their Families: What the Research Tells Us*, *Perspectives on Civil Protective Orders in Domestic Violence Cases: The Rural and*

Urban Divide, and *Nexus Between Economics and Family Violence: The Expected Impact of Recent Economic Declines on the Rates and Patterns of Intimate, Child and Elder Abuse.*

National Network to End Domestic Violence (NNEDV)

2001 S St. NW, Suite 400, Washington, DC   20009
(202) 543-5566 • fax: (202) 543-5626
website: www.nnedv.org

The National Network to End Domestic Violence was formed in 1990 when a small group of domestic violence victim advocates came together to promote federal legislation related to domestic violence. The network led efforts to pass the landmark Violence Against Women Act (VAWA) of 1994. Today, NNEDV provides training and assistance to its state and territorial coalitions in their fight against domestic violence. It also furthers public awareness of domestic violence and hopes to change beliefs that condone intimate partner violence. On its website NNEDV provides links to its current projects, fact sheets on domestic violence, news, and local resources.

Stop Family Violence

331 West Fifty-Seventh St., Suite 518, New York, NY   10019
website: www.stopfamilyviolence.org

The goal of Stop Family Violence is to amplify the nation's collective voice against family violence by empowering people to take action at the local, state, and national level to ensure safety, justice, accountability, and healing for people whose lives are affected by domestic violence. The organization believes that broad social change will not occur simply from well meaning efforts of a few agencies, nor as the result of legislation or education alone. Stop Family Violence therefore hopes to be a catalyst for diverse people to come together and raise their voices to work for social change. Articles available on its website include "Now You See It, Now You Don't: The State of the Battered Women's Movement" and "Human Rights Framework for Addressing International Violence Against Women."

US Department of Justice, Office of Violence Against Women

145 N St. NE, Suite 10W.121, Washington, DC   20530
(202) 307-6026 • fax: (202) 305-2589
website: www.ovw.usdoj.gov

The US Department of Justice, Office of Violence Against Women (OVW) provides federal leadership to reduce violence against women, dating violence, sexual assault, and stalking. The office also administers Violence Against Women Act grants to state, local, tribal, and nonprofit entities that respond to violence against women. OVW publications about domestic violence and teen dating violence can be found at the National Criminal Justice Reference Service website identified above. The OVW website publishes fact sheets about domestic violence and teen dating violence, the Violence Against Women Act, the Violent Crime Control and Law Enforcement Act, and related legislation.

Bibliography of Books

Douglas A. Brownridge — *Violence Against Women: Vulnerable Populations.* New York: Routledge, 2009.

Ricardo Carrillo and Jerry Tello, eds. — *Family Violence and Men of Color: Healing the Wounded Male Spirit.* New York: Springer, 2008.

Richard L. Davis — *Domestic Violence: Intervention, Prevention, Policies, and Solutions.* Boca Raton, FL: CRC Press, 2008.

Walter S. DeKeseredy — *Violence Against Women: Myths, Facts, Controversies.* Toronto: University of Toronto Press, 2011.

Norman J. Finkel — *Emotions and Culpability: How the Law Is at Odds with Psychology, Jurors, and Itself.* Washington, DC: American Psychological Association, 2006.

Aruna Goel, Manvinder Kaur, and Ameer Sultana, eds. — *Violence Against Women: Issues and Perspectives.* New Delhi, India: Deep & Deep, 2006.

Angela J. Hattery — *Intimate Partner Violence.* Lanham, MD: Rowman & Littlefield, 2009.

Karen Heimer and Candace Kruttschnitt, eds. — *Gender and Crime: Patterns of Victimization and Offending.* New York: New York University Press, 2006.

Malcolm Hill, Andrew Lockyer, and Fred Stone, eds. — *Youth Justice and Child Protection.* Philadelphia: J. Kingsley, 2007.

Nicky Ali Jackson, ed. — *Encyclopedia of Domestic Violence.* New York: Routledge, 2007.

Holly Johnson, Natalia Ollus, and Sami Nevala — *Violence Against Women: An International Perspective.* New York: Springer, 2008.

Paula K. Lundberg-Love and Shelly L. Marmion, eds. — *"Intimate" Violence Against Women: When Spouses, Partners, or Lovers Attack.* Westport, CT: Praeger, 2006.

Elizabeth A. Mansley — *Intimate Partner Violence: Race, Social Class, and Masculinity.* El Paso, TX: LFB Scholarly, 2009.

Paul Nathanson and Katherine K. Young — *Legalizing Misandry: From Public Shame to Systemic Discrimination Against Men.* Montreal: McGill-Queen's University Press, 2006.

Laura L. O'Toole, Jessica R. Schiffman, and Margie L. Kiter Edwards, eds. — *Gender Violence: Interdisciplinary Perspectives.* New York: New York University Press, 2007.

Claire M. Renzetti and Raquel Kennedy Bergen — *Violence Against Women.* Lanham, MD: Rowman & Littlefield, 2005.

Stella M. Resko   *Intimate Partner Violence and Women's Economic Insecurity*. El Paso, TX: LFB Scholarly, 2010.

Lee E. Ross, ed.   *The War Against Domestic Violence*. Boca Raton, FL: CRC Press, 2010.

Susan M. Sanders   *Teen Dating Violence: The Invisible Peril*. New York: Peter Lang, 2003.

Natalie J. Sokoloff, ed.   *Domestic Violence at the Margins: Readings on Race, Class, Gender, and Culture*. New Brunswick, NJ: Rutgers University Press, 2005.

Jacquelyn W. White, Mary P. Koss, and Alan E. Kazdin, eds.   *Violence Against Women and Children*. Washington, DC: American Psychological Association, 2011.

Paula Wilcox   *Surviving Domestic Violence: Gender, Poverty, and Agency*. New York: Palgrave Macmillan, 2006.

Katherine van Wormer and Albert R. Roberts   *Death by Domestic Violence: Preventing the Murders and Murder-Suicides*. Westport, CT: Praeger, 2009.

Index